Unified Marketing Strategy

Unite Your Marketing, Advertising, Sales Messaging, and Customer Experience Touchpoints.

Jimmy LaSalle

For general information about on our other products and services, or for technical support, please contact us via email: jim.lasalle@keeninsites.com.

Cover Design: JLaSalle Enterprises + Keen Insites Staff

Credits for cover photos: Heather Eisenberg Photography

Printed in The United States of America

Visit our websites: JimmyLaSalle.com, KeenInsites.com

Library of Congress Control Number: 2021904226

ISBN: 978-1-7366860-2-7 Paperback

ISBN 978-1-7366860-1-0 eBook

Dedication

For my Mom and Dad - You sacrificed so much for your children, and stressed the importance of family, education, and hard work. Thank you for your time, patience, and love.

To my son and daughter, in the event you ever want to know what I did, and how I operated, here you go.

Acknowledgments

Writing a book is harder than I thought it would be, but more rewarding than I imagined once through the undertaking. I do not know that this would have been possible without the occasional get together with my friend Dr. Daniel Camillery. Three years ago, we started discussing our respective book ideas and decided to get together quarterly to have a drink, cigar, and discussions on progress and general self-development. Not only was it helpful to keep going, but I believe we have developed a special bond and learned a little something about each other's determination and drive.

To my clients presently and over the years, the things that I learned from all of you have not only helped me help you, but have helped me have some success as an entrepreneur. A lot of the analogies and information in this book were inspired by you all. I had to get the creative juices flowing to find ways to teach you the similarities between what you had always done and the digital space over the years, and how it will help your respective businesses grow.

A special note to Erran Kagan, whose Jordache Jeans story helped me get through the hyper-growth phases that Driven Local went through and some other times where that shared story was applicable. It taught me that if you have the business, the rest can be figured out. You were a great listener and gave sage advice.

To my friend Rob Nikc, the post production MVP, and a man who can make just about anything a prop for a good story. Thank you for taking the time to go through the book and make the final, final, final edits.

To my former partners at Driven Local, especially Kevin Szypula, whose idea Driven Local was originally. The free time in going my own way after we sold the firm has allowed me all the time I needed to hunker down and get this done. That is, between all of the nice days where I would go and play golf, build my new business, Keen Insites, write a couple of screenplays, learn all about video production, and create my YouTube series, Stories of the Ink, as well as launch the US History Repeated Podcast with my sister Jeananne. You know how I like to keep busy!

Seriously though, thanks for being a good fellow captain on that ship!

Lastly, but always first in my heart, to my amazing wife Laurie. You have put up with me for over twenty years, and your support throughout this journey is greatly appreciated. You never had a problem with me going to meet up with the aforementioned Dr. Dan for one of our 'inspiration sessions,' my working from the bar at my 'GC Office', nor my going to play golf or whatever I did to keep my mind clear to continue moving forward.

If it were not for you, I would not have been able to accomplish all these things. Thank you for everything you do on the homestead and for the children. You are the best Chief Operations Officer any CEO could ask for! I love you.

About the Author

Jimmy LaSalle is a serial entrepreneur with several startups, a successful digital marketing firm called Keen Insites, and former partner in powerhouse marketing firm 'Driven Local.' In 2012, Jimmy and his partners' hard work brought the company national recognition by making it to Inc. Magazine's Fastest Growing 500 privately held companies. You can visit him online at www.jimmylasalle.com or on Twitter (@JimmyLaSalle2)

With the processes outlined in Unified Marketing Strategy, he shares the formula that helped make his clients and his businesses successful.

Contents

Page Left Blank Intentionally

Chapter 1
The Road That Got Me Here

The most successful CEOs and entrepreneurs discovered and embraced the power of marketing. They have the confidence to tell the story of their brand, its strengths and purpose. They have regularly embraced technological advancements and have taken advantage of new marketing tools such as digital marketing. This has helped their businesses adapt to today's world and maintain their success.

I wanted to write a book that would help business owners get a better understanding of the complete marketing picture. A Unified Marketing Strategy connects advertising messages and expectations to your sales team, and customer support. The goal is to choreograph everything and build a powerful system that keeps new customers flowing through the business.

Unified Marketing Strategy was written to help business owners build successful systems within their organization. It will help CEOs instruct and follow up with the C level executives on big picture things to keep in mind for their organizations. It will also help marketing and advertising professionals further develop their media planning.

Unified Marketing Strategy will explain how to bridge all customer experience touchpoints from Advertising to Sales, to Operations and post-sale follow up.

So, you've picked up this book. You may be asking yourself *'Who is Jimmy LaSalle, how can he help me, and why should I listen to him?'* Let me tell you what I do, and how my knowledge can benefit you.

In 2012, a company I was a partner in made it to Inc. Magazine's Fastest Growing 500 privately held companies. Our company 'Driven Local' debuted at #348. Then we made the Inc. Magazine 500/5000 list for three consecutive years, showing up at #709 in 2013, and #1509 in 2014, respectively.

The three plaques received from Inc Magazine that we proudly hung on our wall at Driven Local.

My original four partners and I took a small startup and grew it into a supercharged, digital marketing powerhouse with 80 full-time employees, and over $20,000,000 in gross revenue. It did, however, take a good amount of learning, experimenting, and training to earn the title of "master marketer".

Some relevant personal highlights: I was born in Brooklyn, New York on Jan 13th, 1974.

I grew up in a house of seven, and we shared one bathroom. I tell you this because this is where my training began. My siblings and I were loud, very loud. I learned then how to be heard over the crowd, hold people's attention and be concise with my message, or else I'd run the risk of the audience (our parents) losing interest or getting distracted. These talents come in handy to this day.

I learned from an early age that if I wanted 'extras', I would need to be able to pay for them myself. Subsequently, I got a paper route at the ripe young age of twelve. The soliciting of new customers and the need to follow up for weekly collecting started the early development of my sales skills. So, growing up the way I did, a strong work ethic and a sense of responsibility came naturally to me. I was opportunistic by always trying to make some extra money shoveling snow in the winter and raking leaves for neighbors in the fall.

It took me a few years to realize that hard work, while noble, was inefficient. I needed a way to streamline my entire working process. I had to be smarter about how I worked. So, at the age of 14 I utilized my mom's network to get a job at the church rectory, but truth be told, there was not all that much to do.

There were small projects that came up, but I was mostly answering the phone or handling parishioners that came in for mass cards or wanting to speak with one of the priests. There was always free time, so I was able to complete my homework while getting paid for it. That was pretty sweet. I was also able to read quite a bit while "working". While employed at the Church rectory, I picked up another essential life skill, customer service.

Working hard and smart was not enough. At the age of seventeen, a friend asked me to help him 'DJ' a party. He had the equipment; he just needed some help carrying it and getting the crowd excited. I had not the slightest idea how to dance, or how to get a crowd excited about dancing, but I was never one to back down from a challenge. I agreed to help my friend. I came home quite worried that day since this was entirely new to me. My sister Suzanne took pity and taught me the electric slide, so I knew how to do something on the dance floor.

The DJ thing was probably one of the first times I 'put myself out there,' as they say. I took a chance. Partly to help a friend, and to get better at being social. I was already a marketer in the making by then. I had to work on my social skills, and even though I did not know it yet, this was my first introduction to some of the skills I needed most.

I was a quiet boy growing up. No, I was not shy or afraid of interacting with people, but I liked to retreat into my thoughts and not bother with people unless they bothered with me first. I also was not very comfortable in my skin. I was five foot ten and weighed 130 pounds. As a tall and skinny boy, I was teased by my friends in school and siblings about the way I looked. I donned baggy clothes to look more filled out. Now, try and imagine me dancing. I was a brave young man for agreeing to step out of my comfort zone and attract attention to myself while trying to hype up a crowd, but hey, I ended up finding my rhythm ... eventually!

The following year, when I turned eighteen, I got tired of being the skinny kid and decided to do something about it. I needed to work on a change for the better, so I decided to join a gym with two of my high school friends. The first workout I did was designed by my friend's ex-girlfriend's father, who was a bodybuilder. I threw up afterward, having overdone it, but I didn't give up that day; what does not kill us, makes us stronger, right? Anything worthwhile is not easy. If getting in good shape were easy, everyone would be in good physical condition and we would be a planet of world-class athletes with hot physiques.

I continued hitting the gym and a funny thing happened. I got addicted to it. I have maintained that habit ever since.

I realized that I was always striving to be better, and in reading I found this Japanese term called 'Kaizen'. This word doesn't have a direct English translation; however, it essentially means the 'continuous striving for perfection'. 'Kaizen' essentially expresses the desire to always be better and to always improve on oneself.

I have come to embrace that term and even made it the first Core Value at my organization. It is made up of two words, 'Kai', meaning change, and 'Zen', meaning good. Together, they make "the constant striving for perfection".

At twenty-three, I graduated from St. John University with a bachelor's degree in Finance. I was fortunate enough to get an academic scholarship to SJU. I started in Accounting but felt like the courses were sucking the personality out of me, so I switched to Finance. That cost me an extra semester. That was an acceptable trade and has worked out for me.

Upon graduation, I turned down positions at Goldman Sachs and the US SEC to take a sales job at ADP. Now, many people around me called that an unwise move but I had my reasons. In college I attended a seminar where successful business owners discussed what it was they felt made them successful. The two most valuable skills they picked up were Sales and Leadership skills. Those two jobs that I turned down had higher base salaries, but this sales job offered me an opportunity to formally learn how to generate revenue. I knew my income would grow faster in the sales role than in the other more "prestigious" opportunities I was offered. I didn't care for the prestige, because I knew that improvement is the ultimate power. Once I learned how to generate revenue, I would always be able to make a living and not rely on anyone else. Think of it as modern-day hunting. You can eat what you kill. You can provide.

Most entrepreneurs will agree with me that developing an expertise in sales is possibly the most important skill they picked up. It is also one of the hardest to master. There is a lot to overcome in learning how to sell / generate revenue; first and foremost will be your ability to deal with rejection. We will dive into this later.

Each prospect is a different person with their own unique interests, limitations, needs, and thresholds. You can't possibly treat them all the same way and expect the same result every time. You have to tweak your approach by being able to understand both verbal and non-verbal communication, and more. The sales training I picked up at ADP became part of my DNA. The ability to generate revenue is a skill that allows for true financial freedom if you can master it. I'm not saying I am a "master," but I am always working at it ('Kaizen!').

No one's born knowing good sales techniques, but we are born with the ability to move others to action. Babies cry to let their parents know they need something. Children can get their parent's attention. Sales and Marketing follow the same process. There will be more on this later. All I am saying is that with the proper training and attitude, anyone can become a good salesperson. Sure, some people may be more charming than others and COULD have a slight advantage, but I do not always find that to be the case. In fact, I have had poor experiences as a sales manager with salespeople who rely on their personality, charm, looks, etc., and do not follow a process. This failure on their part limits them to staying average, in my opinion.

Having a process to fall back on makes selling easier while learning because it takes away much of the guessing of what comes next in the conversation. If you want to become a true sales master, you will certainly need a sales process and continue to read, refine, and adapt. There are books on personality types and how to better communicate with certain types of people. Find books you like and read!

'Kaizen' is a journey, not a destination. Keep working at it. I will share the sales processes I have developed and refined later on for you to consider adopting.

I was a salesperson at ADP from January 1997 through November 1999. I had a good manager who taught me how to set goals and rewarded me for achieving them. I recall for the fiscal 99 year, we reviewed my sales & income goals, and what I needed to do to make the President's Club trip. My reward to myself upon achieving the goals was to buy a nice pair of Revo Sunglasses and an engagement ring for my girlfriend.

That year, I qualified for President's Club, bought the pair of sunglasses I had my eye on, and got engaged to the love of my life who is now my wife of almost 20 years! A little more on this later, but I will say that my constant request for feedback drives her mad at times, and yet, she puts up with me.

Note** We will definitely be talking about business goals later, how to set them, how to create a marketing plan around them, and the execution thereof!

At 25, I started on the path to an MBA, which was also at St. John's University. I managed to get ADP and a future employer in the Yellow Page business to pay for my master's degree - mostly.

After a year or so I found myself working in the new .com world. Startups were giving away free money, and then the bubble burst. I was unemployed. I was in the middle of my master's degree program and needed a J-O-B that would allow me the flexibility of carrying on my studies, make a decent income to pay for a wedding, and also allow me to continue to develop Leadership Skills. It is one thing to read up on the great leaders of the business world; it is entirely different to be able to put their principles into practice.

I chose to work for Yellow Book USA, an independent yellow page publisher in New York, out of Long Island. When I started there in 2001, they had 350 directories in 19 states and an aggressive expansion plan that would allow me to grow and learn. Over the next eight years, they would end up having over 1000 directories in 50 states. It was here that I initially learned about advertising, specifically Direct Advertising. This is something we will talk more about later when putting together your marketing plan! I completed my MBA in May 2003 in the field of Marketing.

I started in sales and quickly became an "Associate Sales Manager" where I still sold but also trained and learned how to manage other people on a smaller scale. The company started expanding into simple digital media offerings that were beginning to turn some heads in the advertising world. I continued to learn and take on additional responsibilities. I was doing sales training, leading my small team, and continuing to sell. I was offered a promotion to become a full 'Sales Manager.' I turned it down, for the simple reason that the job was in Manhattan, which would mean a two-hour long commute, (my current commute was a 10-minute drive from my home) and on top of that a twenty thousand dollar pay cut from my current income. I did not see the win; I thanked them for the consideration and told them to let me know when there was an opening in my current office.

The big boss was not happy when I turned it down, but I told him that my wife and I wanted to enjoy as much time together while it was just us while we could, meaning, no children just yet. I couldn't simply tell him that *"I am not taking a $20,000 pay cut to have a commute 2 hours longer, work more hours, and lose all my free time "out in the field",* right?

The next year, in 2004, there was an opportunity in my location. Despite the pay cut, which I negotiated to not to be as awful, I took it. I gave myself a two-year window where it would catch up to where my earnings were at that moment. I subsequently got promoted to what they called a Canvass Manager in 2005, then moved into the more formal Regional Manager position in late 2006. I was able to navigate the new digital landscape much better than the existing management team, and the opportunities started finding me.

Google had only recently brought the idea of search engine marketing to the world. It was so transparent! It was easy to see the powerful results it generated without having to dig too deeply. I fell in love with it.

Around 2007, a friend of mine and I started developing websites on the side. The companies we were working for did not offer websites at the time, and the sales team was looking to get websites created for their clients so that they could try this new Google Pay Per Click (PPC) advertising. I even made one for the current VP when he heard I was doing this on the side to supplement my income. In late 2008 I incorporated under Keen Insites Internet Services Ltd. I was doing about two websites a month and started making some extra money part-time. We found that the biggest error many small businesses faced with their website design was that they were not integrating important information that would help them get the calls from potential customers. We were able to incorporate essential factors (RASCIL) that would help them succeed with their online efforts. More on these factors later!

Also in 2008, a business acquaintance approached me with an idea. He proposed we break out and start our own digital agency along with a few other people. Between the two of us, we had enough knowledge and hands-on experience with sales, backend production, and operations to start. There were four of us at the time, and each of us got a few clients to beta test. As we grew, we created processes and procedures. With the number of digital media strategies, I put together, we got pretty good at translating the client's goals to a digital marketing plan that would be effective for them. We did not take a cookie-cutter approach like many of the larger companies in the space. Instead, we offered customized solutions, tailor-made for each of our clients. Granted, that took a lot of time, but we had developed a ridiculously high, like 95%+ annualized retention rate.

That's the story of how I became a leading voice in the digital marketing and advertising arena. With this book, I hope to give you the tools and techniques to make success happen for you. We will be discussing the strategies used to bring about great results for our clients, the sales processes I use that will hopefully help you onboard the leads you generate from your marketing strategy, as well as the customer experience processes we integrated that allowed for that 95% retention rate! You will find everything you need to know about segmenting your business offerings, creating goals, creating effective website content, and many advanced techniques you may want to add into your plan at a later time.

We will also be providing a simplified overview on marketing and advertising and discussing the more popular types of digital media being used today, setting proper budgets, and more! Once you have read and embraced the content of this book, I promise you will be able to use the strategies and tactics to grow your business and maximize its profits!

Chapter 2
Our Process and Experience

Our Experience

Throughout my career, I have dealt predominantly with small to mid-sized businesses. (SMBs) I have also dealt with large advertising agencies, enterprise level businesses and big brands, but to be fair, 80% + have been what they call SMBs.

My goal is to always help clients achieve their advertising and marketing goals. However, during my Automatic Data Processing (ADP) days I did a lot more. Business owners often called upon me to strengthen their core processes and activities. I also helped streamline their time and attendance processes and eliminated their liability for payroll tax filings as ADP took on the responsibility.

I learned quite a lot as well. For starters, I understood that while no two businesses are alike, they still have similarities. Being a business owner is a difficult undertaking. It involves many sleepless nights, HR dilemmas, financial issues, and management-related problems. However, I have yet to meet a true entrepreneur who'd willingly give up on the trials and troubles of business ownership.

Many business owners would love to leave a mark in their respective fields, but few manage to do that. Most of them live a life of relative ambiguity, struggling to make ends meet. That is where I come in.

My first question to them is, "So how did you get into this business?"

The answers I have received have always been interesting. I learn about the 'why' or 'how' they came to be in this place. Basically, why they chose their fields and what motivated them.

In the world of Yellow Pages, I met with a variety of marketers, managers, and entrepreneurs. They brought their own marketing strategies to the table. They knew what worked for them, and just as importantly, what did not work for them and why! It is just as important to know both because strategies that did not work in the past, may work in the future. Failing happens. When one fails they learn something didn't work; this is vastly different from failure, which is "throwing in the towel" and giving up. Failing allows room for learning, growth and ultimately success will hopefully occur before your cash/ willpower runs out. Failing occurs because it was done incorrectly, or it may have been a matter of poor messaging, but we will not allow failure to be the end result. Think Thomas Edison who was fired from his first two jobs, and then made 1000 unsuccessful attempts at inventing the light bulb!

I continued to ask them about their business. While my ambitions motivated me to ask these questions, as I intended to go into business for myself one day, it also served another essential purpose. I was talking *with them, about them.* Instead of just selling them another ad program, I was getting to *know them.* They appreciated my honesty, and that resulted in good business.

Back in those days, Yellow Pages was the "only game in town" as it pertained to direct advertising. Digital marketing was unheard of back then.

I did my best to help my clients use the Yellow Pages for maximum effectiveness. I helped them put together short-term marketing strategies that went well beyond the realm of YP and helped them grow their businesses. They trusted my advice and often came to discuss any marketing issues that perplexed them. They were looking for a person who was invested in their success, and not just looking to line his/her own pockets. This working relationship was a two-way street; I learned so much from them as well. At the time it was fun. Who knew I was getting ready for a long and illustrious career in the marketing realm?

The Yellow Pages Directory can be called the original "Search Engine". People do not go to the directory unless they need some "direction". This means they kind of know what they are looking for, but they do not know where to get it. It was because of this that I worked very closely with business owners in differentiating their business vs. the competition in their market. We worked on messaging, calls to action, layout, and what things they should have in their copy to "get the calls". We will get into much more detail on this later and how your website works as an electronic storefront for you - AND should be working to generate new business 24 hours a day, today and every day!

Digital marketing was still in its infancy, but I realized businesses with a website demanded attention. A website at least heightened people's interests, and they went online trying to learn more. I encouraged my clients to create websites because they can potentially be an effective method of generating new business 24-

hours a day. I stand by that fact to this day. Here are just some reasons your business needs an effective website:

- In today's day and age, a website builds credibility.

- It acts as an electronic storefront and is probably one of the first impressions you make on your potential clients.

- A website means that you have a direct and straightforward route to communicating with your customers. Therefore, you immediately improve your customer service.

- It always makes your business accessible. A website works to market your business even when you are sleeping.

- It targets larger markets. It doesn't matter if you are providing products or services; an online website is an alternative location to sell them. You can reach clients in another town or country by having a web presence.

- It is a medium to showcase your work. You can have an online portfolio, image gallery, and customer reviews.

- It is a time saver, for both the customer and yourself. You don't have to take your product from your warehouse to a storefront, and your customer need not walk around for hours before purchasing something. "Studies show that once a consumer knows what they need or want, they research, and 72 percent of them go online to find educational material, reviews, and testimonials", according to a recent buyer journey report.[1]

- It allows you to stay current. A web presence is a great platform to help you stay modern. You can update your information and add or remove items at the click of a button. Whether it's breaking news or the latest trend, if you're swift, you can beat your competition and release it first.

- It helps you beat the competition. Many business owners look to the "do it yourself" method of getting a website done instead of hiring a professional. If you have a great website that offers a unique experience to the user, you will get an edge on the market at the expense of your competition.

- A 2015 study by Verisign reports, '84% consumers believe that small businesses with websites are more credible than ones without an online presence. It also concluded that 65% of consumers consider a company branded email to be more credible than a generic email account such as Gmail, Outlook.com or Yahoo mail.'[2]

That last bullet point should resonate with many small business

---

[1] https://www.leadium.io/blog/what-is-the-buyers-journey

[2] https://blog.verisign.com/getting-online/verisign-2015-online-survey-97-percent-of-smbs-would-recommend-having-a-website-to-other-smbs/

owners. If your business email is a Yahoo, Gmail, AOL etc., please update your email. It should be at your domain. It should come with cloud storage too. So, if your email address is anytownroofing@gmail.com go fix it. These are just some benefits of having a website and proper digital set up, and how it helped my clientele gain an edge on the market.

I have gained over twenty years of advertising experience. During this time, I have seen businessmen who had zero internet presence become dominant players online. On the other hand, I have also witnessed successful businesses that did not transition, go bankrupt. You want to be part of the former group.

Take, for example, the way Blockbuster Video died away as Netflix practically took over our lives. In 2000, Reed Hastings, the CEO of Netflix, tried selling his company to Blockbuster for a mere $50 Million. John Antioco, who was the CEO and founder of Blockbuster, refused the offer multiple times. They laughed Hastings out of Blockbuster's conference rooms numerous times. By 2002, however, Netflix was showing signs of potential. It had racked up almost $150 Million in revenues, possessing a 36% profit margin! They sold online, got to the customers faster, and delivered quality entertainment to them in their homes. They didn't even have to wear their pants to see the latest movies! Thus began the downfall of the biggest video rental company in the United States, Blockbuster. Blockbuster closed its last outlet in 2013 and declared bankruptcy. Netflix is now worth $43 Billion. Who is laughing now?

I can tell you one thing with complete certainty, although you have heard it several times throughout your life by now. There is only one constant, and that is change. The digital world is changing fast. New bells, whistles, targeting tactics, marketing avenues and social media sites can translate into more sales for you. Or they can mean the death of your business if you refuse to keep up.

Today's new buzzwords are 'machine learning', 'AI' (Artificial Intelligence), 'Omnichannel', etc. You should avoid 'click-bait', and still get your business 'ranked'. This is just a sampling of the 'lingo' used when referring to internet-related technologies. However, not all of it applies to you. We'll discuss some important ideas that relate to digital marketing, in ensuing chapters.

Throughout my career, I have put together Digital Strategies for all types and sizes of clients. For example, in 2012, I helped Aruba.com clean up their SEM (Search Engine Marketing) campaign. They were bidding on over twenty thousand terms, many of which were terrible. They even had the name of a murder victim as their keyword! The only explanation I found for this was that someone was asleep at the wheel and started blindly copying/pasting terms from analytics programs into their keyword list as soon as they woke up.

We were brought in by their Agency of Record (AOR) to manage their SEM campaign. We were primarily tasked to increase their Click Through Rate (CTR) and lower their Cost-Per-Click. (CPC) We did this by eliminating about eighteen-thousand useless terms.

Later, I also helped Batman and Superman with their marketing! Okay, so I helped a friend at DC Comics put together a small campaign to promote their downloadable stories on the Comixology App. I have always been a comic book nerd, so this was a proud moment for me.

I continue to work with racing venues like Daytona, Talladega, Watkins Glen, Darlington, and Martinsville. We help them

20

promote NASCAR and other racing events. Then there were brands like Lunesta, Chocolate Milk, Tiger Woods Foundation and many others that needed help in creating digital strategies. Often, we were brought in us as a trusted digital partner by prestigious ad agencies.

I can say I have put together hundreds of digital strategies for small and mid-sized businesses. Sometimes I dealt with the client directly; other times, I was helping one of the sales reps in my office, or within our company, or one of our agency partners.

At Driven Local we worked with local businesses and also became successful in the franchise space. We acquired a company in 2013 that had an excellent reputation for client service in the franchise space. I tagged along to a few IFC conferences, learned from my new peers, and started helping some national brands come up with ideas to expand their businesses. Franchise Brands are interested in 3 things:

1. Increasing the Number of Franchisees
2. The Success of the Franchisee
3. The Building of their Brand

I was also involved in the Franchise B2B space by helping a company called 'Franchise Gator' lower their cost-per-lead in Google Adwords. This was accomplished by integrating some new Google Adwords Beta programs. We had access to these beta programs as we were one of the earlier Premier SMB (Small and Medium-Sized businesses) Google Adwords Partners.

My basic strategy has always been to test out the latest and greatest tactics without fear. We do a test run with a small budget to see if it works for them – or sometimes show them it will not work!

Over the years, I have developed a comprehensive process for helping businesses compete online. It starts with breaking down what they do, who they do it for and how to best get in front of those people.

Any business owner can use this process to gain a deeper understanding of how buying occurs. We'll explore how to get your customer's ATTENTION, provide them with timely INFORMATION, stoke their DESIRE, and move them to ACTION. We will also discuss the pros and cons of the mainstream digital media, and how to make it work for you most efficiently. Using this process, anyone can come up with an effective marketing strategy.

After that we will go through the 6 steps of the sale that I picked up in my ADP days and have applied to just about everything I do. This includes the very important module on overcoming objections that will help you convert your marketing targets from prospects to customers.

Lastly, we will have you work on what you want your customers to experience. How do you set the proper expectations without overpromising and under delivering?

I'm hoping you will embrace planning all of this out, and like Hannibal Smith would say, "I LOVE it when a plan comes together!"

- Business Analysis
- How Customers Find You
- Customer Buying Process
- Create Marketing Plan
- Sales Processes Choreographed
- Customer Experience Management

I LOVE IT WHEN A PLAN COMES TOGETHER

We will focus on the six areas above. Ready to get started?

Chapter 3
Business Analysis

Now that I have introduced myself and have shed sufficient light on how I gained experience in the digital advertising industry, it is time to move toward the essence of the book. Let us take one step at a time and go through the first step a business needs to go through before we are able to strengthen its marketing and sales.

The most important step in creating a marketing plan is to understand the "current state" of the business, i.e., where you are now vs. the "desired state" of the business, i.e., where you want to be in six months, twelve months, and the years to come.

You need to know where you are as well as where you want to get to.
https://blogs.articulate.com/rapid-elearning/heres-an-easy-way-to-create-learning-objectives/

I do this by delving into the history of the company because it tells how the organization got to where it stands today. The history helps me as a digital advertiser/marketer determine the most plausible marketing plan for any given enterprise.

The current state of a business is a snapshot of where it stands today. We do a SWOT analysis and identify all the current strengths, weaknesses, opportunities, and threats. We dig into the numbers. We dig into processes. We want to get a true and fair view of how the business is performing. Based on that, you can set goals for the future and pave the way to the desired state.

The goal of this book is to help you put together a plan that helps your business get to the point where you want it to be. For that, we are going to use this chapter as a little workshop. So, if you want to create a great marketing plan, take all the time you need to go deep into the answers to the questions I posed.

In the Appendix of this book, we incorporated a worksheet for you to jot down answers, provided space to flesh out thoughts, and tables to write in data. There is also an electronic version of this spreadsheet at www.jimmylasalle.com.

Asking the right questions can help you accomplish the most seemingly insurmountable goals. You can always read this chapter and come back to refer to it whenever you are ready, but I strongly suggest you take the time to conduct a full business analysis, outline where you want your business to be, so you can then steer it in the right direction. I mentioned in the previous chapter that my all-time favorite question to ask entrepreneurs is, "How did you get into this business?" I like to know what convinced them to pursue a career in the field as I mentioned earlier. Two of the more common answers I get are:

- It was a family business that I got involved in because ... (whatever the reason may be).

- I worked for someone else, saw they were making good money and decided to start my own...

These answers give me an idea on *their* current state, their passion for what they do and, more importantly, provide me with the answer as to "why" they do what they do. There is a very good book by Simon Sinek called 'Start with Why'. You can also find a podcast that sums up the book nicely. The writer, Simon Sinek, and his team perform workshops for companies all around the world helping them find their "why". [3] You can do this on your own with their other book, 'Finding Your Why'. I have read it and think any business owner could benefit from it. Now, let's break down your business and everyone else's into simplest terms. Let's speak to why every business is the same...then we will determine how different your business is. (It won't be!)

All businesses sell something, a product, a service ... *something.*

They sell whatever "it" is for x amount, then they fulfill this something with however they do it, whether manufactured, serviced, shipped, created, etc., - for which there are costs associated, such as cost of goods sold.

Whatever the difference is between the sale price and the cost of goods sold = Profit

While there are many departments within a company, they all stem from 3 general business segments which rely on each other for the complete success of the business. Those segments are:

---

[3] https://simonsinek.com/product/start-with-why/

1 - Sales and Marketing

2 - Operations

3 – Finance

If you rank the health of your Sales/Marketing and Operations on a scale of 1-10, the average score is your Financial Score.

SM Score + Ops Score / 2 = Financial Health of your company on a scale of 1-10.

Ok - what do we mean by this and how can we figure this out? Let's break it down by segment.

First, let's define ranges for 1 - 10 for Sales / Marketing and Operations.

Sales & Marketing

A score of 1 would mean that you have zero new business sales and not enough revenue to pay the bills.

A score of 5 would mean you have plenty of revenue, you are making money, but growth is slow going.

If you score yourself a 10, that essentially means things are almost too good to be true and you can't handle the revenue coming in and you need to turn away business, have a waiting list, or are able to cherry pick the type of clients you want! This is a good position to be in, for sure.

Operations

A score of 1 means your Operations team pretty much ruins every piece of business that comes in, which is obviously not a very good sign.

A score of 5 is when the Operations team can keep up with the Sales department. However, you have concerns and anticipate the problems that would surface if business increased too quickly.

A score of 10 and your Operations team is a well-oiled machine with processes and systems that can run efficiently no matter who is sick, who quits, who is on vacation, etc.

Now, place your business somewhere between 1 and 10 for both departments.

If you rate your Sales & Marketing department an 8 and your Operations team a 6, it means your Financial Score is 7. Similarly, if you rate your Sales & Marketing department 4 and your Operations team 6, in financial terms, you are a 5.

Keep this in mind. This score will provide you with a fair assessment of the current state of your business, which is obviously very important when it comes to setting goals for the future.

So, going back to the standard sales / cost / profit equation we had before:

What you are selling (Sales/Marketing), less cost of goods sold (operations) = Profit

It is then fair to say that in order to increase profit, you can do any of the following:

- Sell MORE units of new business

- ADD additional products or services to sell to existing clientele

- Have operations manage sales more efficiently (CHANGE PROCESSES)

- Lower cost of Sales or Operations

We propose you look at all of these and determine which is right for your business. It can be more than one.

Let's keep in mind that this is a book on developing a marketing strategy to help drive sales (for which we will help you with a process), and then discuss customer experience management (operations) to keep the customer happy. So all of this is relevant and all businesses are the same!

1 – What business do you do?

In response to this question, you need to define all your products and services that your business offers. Not only are you supposed to list all the offerings, but also rank them in terms of importance. Doing so will ascertain the offerings that matter to your business the most and the least. It wasn't until the McDonald's Brothers, Dick and Mac, reduced their menu to burgers, fries and beverages that their business became efficient and truly took off.

2 – Who are your customers?

This is perhaps the most important question to answer. Defining your customer base brings a lot of concerns to your attention. Also, it opens a lot of opportunities for you. Thus, you need to define your customers, the potential problems or needs they have that may have them turning to you or someone like you, i.e. your competitor.

3 – Where do your customers come from?

This question also pertains to your customer base. You need to determine the areas and geographical locations where your customer base comes from. Do they travel to you, or do you travel to them? Put your location on a map and create a heat map of sorts based on customer concentration.

Can you handle expansion and cover more territory?

4 – Why are you good for them? Why should they choose you?

Every business has its strengths. It's time you determine the strengths of your business. You just have to answer a series of pertinent questions, like what sets your business apart from your competitors? What makes you good? It could be your fast service. It could be strong customer support. It could be the professional staff. It could be a superior offering/product.

5 – Who are your competitors? Why would your potential or existing customers choose them? What can you get better at?

Who are your competitors?

What do they do that you like? Perhaps you can learn from your competition!

What do they do better than you?

Why would someone choose one of your competitors over you? Be honest!

What reasons would you list that you can do better - i.e., what do you suck at?? (This is an important question for you to answer.) Sometimes it is very hard to take a look in the mirror and really know what you do wrong.

Ask your staff what you can be doing better. As a business owner, you have to realize that you are not perfect. Every good leader surrounds themselves with smart people. Your team knows your weaknesses, trust me. Ask them.

6 – Getting into the numbers

As mentioned earlier in this chapter, the current business state is a snapshot of how your business is doing.

What gets measured tends to get done, and what gets measured vs. goals tends to improve. Put together some key performance indicators like:

- Gross Revenue last year, and perhaps the year prior as well.

- What is your projected revenue this year?

- How much revenue, as a percentage, is coming from each of your offerings?

- How much profit, as a percentage of gross profit, is coming from each revenue source?

- Is there a loss leader (a product sold at a loss to attract customers)?

- Is there a way to do more of what is MOST PROFITABLE?

7– Operations

In order to best view your operational processes, outline your business workflow in a flowchart. This would clearly show what happens when fulfilling a work order.

What are your operations and processes, and is everything documented or not?

You need to outline each operational process of your business and how you want it to be done.

Create a flowchart of what happens from beginning to end, from the time a customer calls to the time they pay and tell you they will refer business to you in the future!

Note: Referrals happen after you have done a good job AND someone mentions to your client that they are looking for a service that your company provides. That's when your client remembers you and recommends your services, and not sooner. You can't force a referral.

What you can do is stay in communication with clients by regularly trying to educate and keep them informed on social media, or as part of your email marketing campaign. Staying top of mind is great and is also a good branding play. More detail on this later on.

Here is an interesting operational question to ponder: What is your current capacity to bring on more business?

Make sure you answer this question realistically. You don't want to spend a boatload of money on advertising and not having someone picking up the phone when it rings, or turning people away because you are "too busy."

8 – How do you sell?

It's time to identify what kind of sales processes you have in place. Write down the steps you take to bring on a client and then ask your salespeople what their perception is. Maybe it needs some tweaking. Does your marketing and sales collateral mesh? Is it consistent? We will dive into sales processes at a later time, but document yours now, so that you have a basis for comparison.

9 – What is your current advertising situation?

In order to answer this question, it's best if you make a grid. List all the advertising you are doing currently, the goal of the advertising you're doing, how much you are spending in a month, and the average number of leads it generates.

Underneath, make a list of advertising tactics that used to work for your business. For instance, what advertising platforms you used (yellow pages, trade magazines, print, etc.), how much did you spend in a month, estimate the number of monthly leads, and when and why you stopped spending money on that platform. My guess is that you stopped because of a drop in usage of the media, like Yellow Pages and older print media.

Moreover, if your goal with a tactic is branding, list it as such. Branding advertisements are not supposed to make the phone ring. They aim to keep your product or service on top of your client or potential customer's minds. More on this later; there is a method to the line of questions here!

Now that we have put together data for analyzing the current state of your business, it's time I talked about determining the desired state of your business.

So, let's talk about where we want to get to!

Part 2 - Defining the Desired State - Where are we looking to get to?

Do you want to maintain your current state and perhaps try to improve profitability, or are you looking to grow?

This section is about setting goals and defining where, and by when you want to get there. Let's keep in mind that this is never really a straight line. As business owners, we pretty much know this already. I found this image online and it is pretty accurate.

SUCCESS   SUCCESS

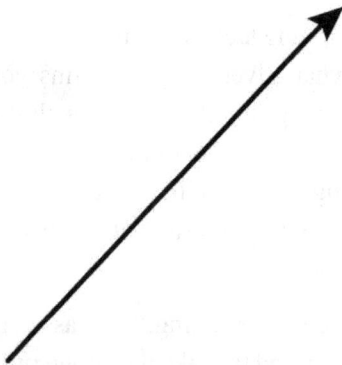

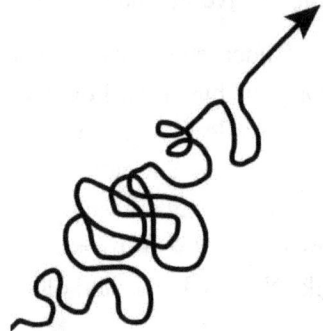

**what people think
it looks like**   **what it really
looks like**

*There are obstacles and unknown turns that need to be navigated. Success is very
rarely a straight line – J LaSalle*
https://beefrunner.com/2018/08/16/consistency-progress-running-training/

Where do you want revenue to be? Is there a product or service you wish to expand into? These questions and more need to be answered.

When analyzing your business to assess its current state, you listed all your products and services and the revenue from each product or service. You should be setting targets and goals going forward for each of these areas.

You need to identify these goals because the way we will plan on allocating your advertising is going to be based off the roadmap we create to get you from the current state to the desired state. This is why we went through the exercise of analyzing the current state.

So, here's what you need to do:

For each of the sections discussed above, make a list of the problems that need to be solved, jot down your business goals, revenue goals, sales goals, and subsequent manpower / hiring / training needs to get to the next level.

Each of the above should be addressed when you are setting targets for your future desired state.

1 – What business do you want to be in? Make a list of products or services to add to or remove from your current offerings, and by when. Set a date!

2 - Who should your customers be? Break out the demographics of your target audience and rank them in importance - who are your best customers? Who are your worst customers?

3 - Where do you want to service? Should you be going further out, or should you be eliminating clients beyond a certain distance because they are too expensive to service?

4 / 5 - Your strengths vs the competition - This section will be important in laying out your messaging to the potential clients in your marketplace. We need to be clear and capitalize on your strengths, and be mindful of where the competition is strong, as well as how you can learn from them to improve. List a few things you will incorporate that your competition is already doing, some things they are not doing, and ways you feel you can outperform them. Make sure anything that needs changing or updating gets listed here with due dates for you or your team.

6 - Know the numbers you wish to achieve

- Gross revenues 1-3 years out

- Number of new business units needed to achieve your revenue goals, then divide by twelve to get the monthly number.

- How much internal growth will your sales team need? Or better yet, how can we increase the daily, weekly, monthly activity of your current team to achieve the new goals without hiring more people? (More on this in the sales process section.)

- What products or services should be of higher or lower focus based off what you found in the current state exercise?

7 - Operational efficiencies - what can be improved? What processes will you change first? Prioritize!

8 - Sales & Marketing Processes: This is how you want things represented in the future. Do this after reading the sales section and / or talking to your team to find best practices currently happening and incorporating them into an adjusted model going forward.

9 - Outline your future advertising and marketing upon completion of the program and incorporate all you learned in the following sections. There is a lot and this will take some time. We will break down several tactics in the following chapters for you to consider incorporating, and identify the proper mix for your business based on your goals.

Before I proceed to the next chapter, I would like to remind you that this is a book on developing an effective marketing strategy to help drive sales (for which I will help you with a process). Then the book will also discuss customer experience management (operations) which is necessary for keeping the customer happy and satisfied.

Are you ready for the next phase?

**If you wish to download this worksheet in order to complete it digitally, please visit JimmyLaSalle.com. I have also included it within the Appendix at the end of the book with accompanying space for you to answer each question.

Chapter 4
How Do Customers Find You?

THOSE WHO KNOW YOU		THOSE WHO DON'T	
✓ Recommended	✓ Passers-by	✓ Newcomers	✓ Infrequent Need
✓ Advertising	✓ Former Customers	✓ Emergency	✓ Comparison Buyers
✓ Solicited		✓ Dissatisfied	✓ Travelers

Businesses continuously gain and lose customers for different reasons

You need to understand that new customers keep your business growing. If you are not generating new clients, then your business is dying. One of the core responsibilities of a business owner is to oversee business development and make sure you continue to build a strong customer base.

The more customers you have, the stronger the foundation of your business. It sounds simple, but your business is going to continuously lose customers, no matter what. That's the harsh reality of running a business that you have to live with. Gaining and losing customers in business is part of the customer life cycle. There are always customers that churn out – sometimes for reasons beyond your control.

Perhaps their credit is not good and they can't meet their financial obligations.

People move away, people pass away.

Some customers begin using alternative products and services and discontinue the use of the product or service that you offer.

There are customers who are dissatisfied with whatever product or service your business offers and, as a result, you lose them.

Some services (think roofing) do not need to be redone for 20-25 years! (Although, if one roof on a street needs to be redone, there is a good chance that other neighbors are prime prospects. We will discuss ideas on how to best target these people later.) So, long story short, there are customers whose need is fulfilled and will not need your services for some time.

Many of these are out of your control, so please realize how important it is to get new customers at a higher rate than you lose them!

In my experience, new customers usually fall into two major categories: Those who know your business and those who don't. First, let's discuss how you gain customers that already know your business and may be familiar with your brand.

Those that know you

- Were recommended to you by another customer
- Pass by your location every day and never had a need, until now
- Have seen your advertising, never had a need for it, but then suddenly they do and realize "I know this person" and "I pass their place every day!"
- Used to come in, i.e., former customers

- You solicited over time from advertising in some form or fashion

Finding "Those who KNOW you"

There can be many ways in which your customers might have already been introduced to your business or the name of your brand before they purchase your product or use your service.

Recommendation

These are people referred to you by others that know you. This happens when in the course of conversation someone mentions that they have a need. People in general do want to be helpful, so when they are able to help someone, they do. This is the most powerful way to get a new customer, through word of mouth. Think, "I have a guy". Customers happy with your service will refer you when the opportunity presents itself, but won't go shouting your praises at random. If, however, they had a bad experience, they will tell everyone they know, without being asked. I am sure you have done this yourself. Everyone likes to share a bad experience. Misery LOVES company!

Passers-By

You don't even realize how many potential customers just pass by your business location every single day. These potential customers just walk or drive by without buying your products or services because they don't have a current need. However, when they do have the need, they may already know your business offerings and become a new customer.

Advertising

A business usually advertises its offerings to its target audience. The rule of thumb is that the more you advertise, the wider the audience you can reach. However, there are countless people who see the advertisements of your business on different platforms and do not pay any attention to them because they don't have a current need. Some advertising tactics introduce your brand to people whether they are looking for your type of business or not. When they are ready, the money spent to brand your business will be well worth it. Name recognition kicks in and they know they heard of you "somewhere".

Former Customers

People who have used your business in the past may have the need for using your product or service again. This means your former customers can possibly turn into your current customers any given day. Needless to say, these customers will be well aware of your business and its offerings because they would have used them before.

Soliciting Customers

Perhaps it was a local event your company attended, perhaps it was the door hanger one of your staff left on a few homes when they were performing work on a particular street. (Great thing to do for roofers, by the way.) In any event, they have been solicited by you in the past and are aware of what you offer. In short, they get to know your business before buying your products or services.

Those that don't know you

- Just moved to the area

- May have an infrequent need

- Are buying something already, but want to compare pricing or features

- Have an emergency; they don't know anyone who can service this issue in the area, but will find one

- Have been dissatisfied with the last person that did work for them; now looking for a replacement since they were not happy

- Are passing through

Finding customers that "DON'T KNOW" you

On the other side of the coin, there are several situations that arise that would allow you to get new customers who have never heard of you.

Just Moved to the Area

When people move to a new home or apartment and don't know the neighborhood, they do not know who is good at what they do. They need everything - restaurants, supermarkets, dry cleaner, etc. How are you getting in front of these new people to your area?

Infrequent Need

How many times do you move? For most people, not that often, and if you move far away and used a local company to move you last time, chances are that you need to find a different moving company should you need to move again. Sometimes the need is so infrequent that the old business owner retires or sells his business. Guess what, that opens a new opportunity!

Price Comparisons

There are people who might be set on purchasing a product or service from someone else. As a way to compare someone else's similar offering to the one they have nearly decided on, they look for a couple of competitors, or solicit a few bids. If they find your brand fits their needs, they may switch their preference and become your customer instead. Perhaps they are shopping for new kitchen cabinets, meet someone at a trade show, they give an estimate, but they want to compare with a few other people to make sure what they have is in line with the rest of the market. Here is a chance to get your hat in the ring! Maybe there is something you can provide that the competitor can't.

Emergency Situations & Services

If you are out of town and you have a problem with your teeth, you're going to find a dentist because you need one. This is an example of an emergency, or "emergency service". It happens more often than you think.

Dissatisfaction

Have you ever experienced being dissatisfied with a particular service and the next time something goes wrong you have called someone else? I have. No one is perfect. Not you, not your competition. Mistakes happen and people become unhappy and move on. Hopefully they decide to move on to you! Will you be ready for them?

People Just Passing By

Sometimes you just happen to gain a customer that was passing by and realized they needed something at that moment. Right place, right time. This is probably the most prevalent with food related purchases. I can't tell you how many times I was hungry and needed to find a place to eat or order food, and move on.

Next chapter starts the discussion on different types of advertising, and we continue to move closer to identifying which tactics are right for your business!

Chapter 5
Advertising Types Explained Creative vs. Direct & Traditional vs. Digital

Advertising has come a long way since the day it was perceived as an important tool to attract customers, build their perception about a product and service, and influence them to buy the advertised offering. The original idea of advertising has remained the same over the years, but the means of advertising has changed drastically. Also, consumer behavior has evolved over time.

Many advertising techniques that were popular 20 or 30 years ago have been rendered obsolete. There was a time when the fundamental tools of advertising were television, radio, billboards, newspapers, and the yellow pages. You can say that the yellow page directory was the world's first search engine! If there was any product or service that people needed to look for, they knew they would find it in the yellow pages. Although TV, radio and billboards are still in use today, there's a world of difference between old school and contemporary advertising.

Today, the advertising industry goes full speed ahead using the most modern, digital tools. That's all because of the advent of the internet – the single most revolutionary invention of the century. It has opened new doors and has brought a wave of change in the advertising industry.

Traditional / Pre-Internet Advertising

Prior to the internet, businesses had no choice but to advertise in only the brick-and-mortar world. If you had a business you would utilize advertising to drive new business either to your storefront, or direct consumers to call and schedule an appointment or consultation. That was the function of the Yellow Pages. People needed a number and an address to reach out to a business that would meet their demands as a consumer, and it used to provide you with just that. That is 'Direct Advertising'.

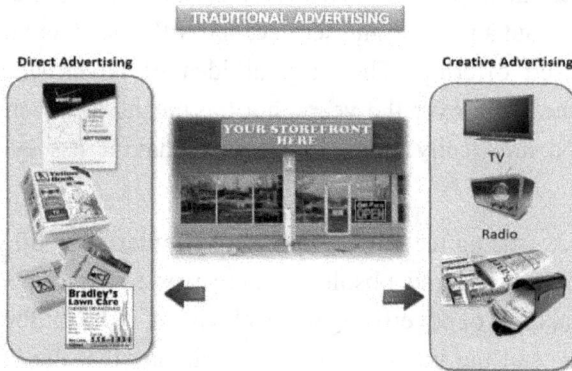

Traditional advertising directed people to a brick-and-mortar storefront.

Similarly, television, radio, or newspaper advertising was a good way of getting your product or service in front of consumers to build awareness in the pre-internet era. This is considered 'Creative Advertising'.

Now, in the internet age, the landscape of the advertising industry has changed; however, the TYPE of advertising has stayed the same and falls into the same two categories – Creative Advertising and Direct Advertising.

Digital Advertising

Digital advertising is unlike anything people imagined advertising would evolve into 25+ years ago. The proliferation of digital advertising can be understood by the importance of a website. Today, a business would have a tough time being successful without a website. A business' website acts as an electronic storefront, and the goal of modern-day advertising is to drive traffic to a business' website and hope that the new visitor eventually becomes a customer.

With digital advertising, a business's website acts as an electronic storefront. The advertisements are made to drive the traffic to the website. This makes the website, in many cases, the first impression you can make on a potential customer.

There are several ways TO advertise, but the communication or type of tactic will be either direct or creative advertising – so let's break down what that means.

Direct Advertising

Direct advertising puts the message in front of people who are looking for a particular product or service but don't know where to get it.

As touched on previously, people would use a Yellow Page directory when they wanted to be DIRECTED to something specific they needed. A lot of times it would be something for emergency service like a plumber, roofer, refrigerator repair, or perhaps an infrequently needed item like a dumpster to rent.

The bottom line is that people would have an idea of what they needed, and would be ready to make a buying decision; they just did not know where to get it or whom they should call. People or "users" would only go to the heading they needed and then return the book to the place they kept it. If they were looking for a window cleaning service, they would *only* look for a window cleaning service. The rest of the ads in the yellow pages would be of no interest to them. People use directories as a reference.

If you were to walk into a building and did not know what floor to go to, most office buildings would have a directory you can use to find the location. I can pretty much guarantee that you are not looking to see who else has an office in the building, right? You find what you are looking for and you are done.

In modern times, the Yellow Pages have been replaced with search engines. Thus, we can conclude that the modern search engine is simply a more comprehensive directory. People go to search engines when they are looking for something specific but don't know where to get it. Again, the Yellow Pages could easily be considered the world's first search engine!

20 years ago, (I would even say through 2007 / 2008) people would pick up the phone book to be directed to where to buy something. It was really the smartphone that gave people immediate access to the internet. Today, you have search engines

– Google, Bing, Yahoo, etc., and you can use these search engines on your phones, tablets, and computers any time you want and anywhere that you can get that connection. So, like "Video Killed the Radio Star", the Search Engines killed the Yellow Pages, encyclopedias, card catalog and anything that you would previously use as a reference or directory source. Want to settle a bet with your friend on who the 3rd baseman was for the Pittsburgh Pirates in 1980? (Note, a quick search yielded Bill Madlock, but Dale Berra played 27 games there in 1980.) How great is it to have everything at your fingertips? For the consumer, it is fantastic! For the business owner? Hmm – how prepared are you to compete online? This is one of the things you will learn in this book.

You will learn how to compete online. Granted I went on a tangent to prove utility and frequency, but the point is that people do not use the search engines unless they are looking for something. There's no casual reading involved here! This is where businesses can get in front of potential customers who are ready to buy.

Creative Advertising

Advertising platforms like TV, radio, billboards, direct mail, and newspapers fall under the category creative advertising. This type of advertising will put your message in front of people who don't necessarily need your product or service currently. Creative advertising is also done on digital platforms. The online tools widely used for creative advertising include remarketing, display ads and banners, social media, video ads, etc. The idea is to put your message in front of users who are likely to need your service in the future, with the hopes that they remember you when they do. If someone has a plumbing problem or a plumbing emergency, they are not going to go turn on the TV or the radio to wait for an advertisement for a plumbing service. Immediate need is for DIRECT advertising. They would go and actively look for a plumber immediately.

So again, Creative advertising helps get the attention of your target market and enhances the awareness of your product or service to that audience. It brings your brand in front of potential customers PRIOR to them having a need. The goal is to make your brand memorable. When they do have a desire for what you offer, they are likely to remember your brand.

Differences between Direct and Creative Advertising

As discussed previously, direct advertising cares for the immediate need. As for creative advertising, it usually has a longer cycle. It prepares people for using products and services in the future by making them aware of what's available in the market.

From an advertiser's standpoint, you, as a business owner, are limited to a certain amount of money that you can spend on direct advertising because there are only a finite number of people "looking" for what you do. The supply and demand ratio has to be kept in perspective before investing in direct advertising.

On the other hand, with creative advertising, you have a potentially limitless ability to spend money. The law of diminishing returns applies to this style of advertising. There is a tipping point where these tactics become ineffective. Consider a billboard that you pass on your way to work each day. You notice it, but you don't read it every day. Guess when you notice that billboard again? When it has changed to another ad, of course! So, while the repetition is good, it eventually can become white noise if there is not any variation to what you do.

When we compare traditional vs digital advertising tactics, you will find that each traditional (real world) advertising has its digital equivalent. The following table will help you understand a little better.

Traditional	Digital
TV	YouTube, Vimeo, Instream Video
Radio	Apple Radio, Pandora, Spotify, etc.
Billboards	Social Media Ads / Display Ads – targeting individuals, but not directing people at that time
Newspaper	Content Targeted Display – when people are reading content
Direct Mail	Email Marketing
Newsletters	Social Media / Blogging
Yellow Pages	Search Engine Marketing (SEM) / Search Engine Optimization (SEO)

Chapter 6
Buying Funnel vs. Media

So now that you have a better understanding of creative and direct advertising types, we are going to take the next step and apply it to the process that everyone goes through when making a buying decision. This is a key component of everything we are trying to accomplish here.

It is important to understand and embrace the fact that people go through a specific process when making a purchase for any product or service. This is universal, and I will provide you examples.

It is important to note that people do not like feeling that they were "sold" on something. People will, however, buy things that they want!

So, the big question is: How do they get to that point?

There is a time-tested process that everyone goes through for all purchases. Sometimes it is a quick process, other times it can be painstakingly slow.

It is a four-step process:

1. Attention

2. Information

3. Desire

4. Action

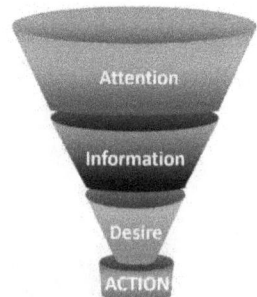

Going through the Buying Funnel

Let's take you through a quick example of someone moving through this **Process.**

Step 1

Situation: You walk into your home and there is water on the floor.

This will *UNDOUBTEDLY* get your *ATTENTION!*

Step 2

You will now naturally follow the water and look to see where it is coming from.

Now apart from Frosty the Snowman making a visit to your home and melting, it is pretty obvious that you have a real problem. You are looking for *INFORMATION.* Perhaps it's coming from the ceiling. (Whew! It's not coming from the ceiling.) You go on to check the bathroom, and see some water coming from under the toilet. You have found your problem!

Step 3:

Now maybe you are the "Mr. Fix-It" type, but let's assume you are not and now know that you need the help of a trained professional. Congratulations, you now have *DESIRE* for the services of a professional plumber.

Step 4

You take *ACTION* and find a local plumber to perform the repairs.

This example shows a very fast movement through the process, but I assure you that it is the same for all products and services. You are going to go through this process mentally, whether you realize it or not.

The plumbing example above was for an emergency type of service. These situations are typically faster than most purchases. Not all things are an emergency, but what you can figure out is the average "sales cycle", the length of time it takes to get a client's attention and move them through this process to become an actual customer. Depending upon your average sales cycle, you will need to adjust the percentages allocated to advertising in respect to these phases.

People ask me, "What about impulse items?"

My answer:

It is UNIVERSAL.

Impulse item: You are standing in line at the supermarket and have zero intention of buying a magazine. You are standing there waiting and looking at the headlines on the magazine rack when one gets your <u>attention</u>. You are curious, (information) perhaps think about picking it up while you are waiting. You want to know (desire). Remember, enquiring minds *want to know*! You are called to the register. Do you take the magazine with you? It happens. That is why they are there. It is very fast from one phase to the next, but this is how the magic happens.

I have trained many salespeople on how to put together media plans and set up specific tactics. I have explained this to all my clients at one time or another. It is at the very core of sales / marketing / advertising. This is how we connect to our prospective clients. Those that get this, are able to be successful. Those that do not grasp this will always struggle in setting up a complete marketing solution. Not all advertising is designed to make the phone ring immediately. Some are designed to get attention, some are designed to get information, some are focused on creating desire, and others are designed to put your business in front of people ready to take action. The next few chapters will break down the different digital media tactics explaining how each work and by showing which are creative, which are direct, which are for attention, information, desire, or action. For now, we are giving a general overview of where they belong on the buying funnel.

See the updated funnel below with Creative Vs Direct overlaid on their respective areas of the funnel.

Revisit Creative and Direct Advertising

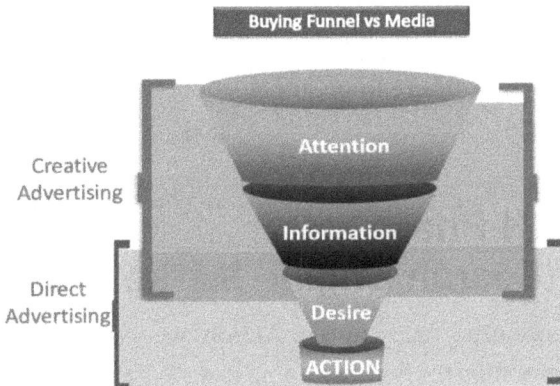

This is how creative vs direct advertising tactics would line up with the funnel. Note the

overlapping on desire.

Creative Advertising proves to be the best for attracting the target audience's attention, providing information, and creating some desire. You will notice an overlap of creative and direct over the desire portion.

Direct Advertising, on the other hand, proves to be the best for reinforcing desire and rousing the target audience to take action!

I usually explain this to business owners in a manner where I go backwards through the process (i.e. Action to Attention) as I want them to understand what each piece does. I always begin with the immediate gratification of making their phone ring or lead generation.

I will summarize many of the tactics here, but worry not, we will dig into each one with more detail in the coming chapters.

There are all these people already looking for what you do, but they don't know where to go to get it. These people are ready to take **action**.

ACTION Phase
SEM (Search Engine Marketing)

For those users ready to take **Action**, we would want to make sure we appear on the Search Engine Results Page (SERP) as often as possible. This is how Google became so big and profitable.

They allowed businesses to purchase ads in a Pay-Per-Click (PPC) manner. It does not matter how many times your ads show, you only incur a fee when the user clicks on your ad and goes to your website. This is called **Search Engine Marketing (SEM)** and should not be confused with **SEO (Search Engine Optimization)**

Users do a **Search** for something specific when ready to take **action.** SEM is helping you grab the **low hanging fruit,** where people are looking for what you do; they just don't know where to go to get it. These ads come up at the very top of the first page of Google results. If your site is not coming up, but your competitors does, who do you think is going to get the business?

SEO (Search Engine Optimization)

I list SEO second up on the immediate gratification scale. SEO is a longer-term process than SEM. SEM can make your phone ring tomorrow, while SEO takes time because it is a process. We will go into SEO in a little more detail, but in a nutshell, you are making changes to your site, its content, and utilizing other external initiatives to have your site appear higher in the SERPs without paying for the traffic generated.

SEM is paying for traffic; SEO is working to get a position. You do not pay for traffic when you get site visitors from your organic listings, but you do have to pay for the work to be done or you can always do it yourself.

Next up would be **online directory listings and reviews**. Still part of the "actionable" section as people may be looking for references, reviews, or a phone number - even from a referral who mentioned your business specifically. If you want a good read, take a look at The Zero Moment of Truth (ZMOT) authored by Jim Lecinski.

"Whether we're shopping for corn flakes, concert tickets or a honeymoon in Paris, the Internet has changed how we decide what to buy. At Google, we call this online decision-making moment the 'Zero Moment of Truth', or simply, ZMOT. The ZMOT refers to the moment in the buying process when the consumer researches a product prior to purchase."[4]

People may have questions or want to compare brands right at the moment prior to purchase. The internet makes that possible. These questions can be anything from 'Which brand of milk will help my kid grow strong and healthy?' to 'What moisturizer will make my skin softer?' or 'What will remove stains from my clothes?' A brand that can answer these types of questions at the right time has a definitive edge. It gains a competitive advantage over other brands.

The ZMOT has become a global behavior. Thanks to the ubiquity of smartphones, these moments are now mobile. Now, search is possible from anywhere at any given time. Meaning, as consumers' behavior has evolved, so must the ways in which brands engage them.

DESIRE Phase

Moving up the funnel, after **Action**, we are now ready to tackle the **Desire** section, which overlap both the direct and creative sections of the funnel.

Remarketing / Retargeting

---

[4] "Zero Moment of Truth (ZMOT) Decision-Making Moment." *Think with Google*. Retrieved from https://www.thinkwithgoogle.com/marketing-resources/micro-moments/zero-moment-truth/

Someone found your site, whether by search, referral, or happenstance in their internet travels as they had some interest in what you do, provide, or sell.

This tactic straddles creative and direct, because if the user got to your site because they were making a buying decision, (looking for something to buy, but not knowing where to get it) but want to compare a few vendors, this tactic will follow them around and remind them to follow up with you specifically when it comes time to pull the trigger on the purchase.

Remarketing ads help you stay top of mind so that when the user moves from **Desire** to **Action** you have a better chance of winning that business. Remarketing is a tactic where the ads seem to follow you around the internet (and they do!).

If the user got to your site because they were looking for **information**, then the retargeting will follow them around and help you stay top of mind and remind them of you.

As an example, have you ever looked at shoes on an e-commerce website, and then, in your browsing travels, you may see that pair of shoes seemingly follow you from site to site? This is what remarketing / retargeting does.

It matters not whether you were actively shopping, or merely browsing. Once that cookie hits your browser, you become their target.

We will share a few different retargeting tactics when we dig into more detail.

These ads will follow your site visitors around and make them feel that it was "meant to be". You may not notice them all the time, but if you pay attention to the ads on the pages you visit, you will be sure to see some very familiar products or services.

The INFORMATION Phase

As we continue to work backwards up the **Buying Funnel** you have other tactics that you can introduce. **Email Marketing** will prompt people for information or remind them that they have been to your website. Email Marketing campaigns are meant to INFORM. An email campaign can be used to send a regularly scheduled newsletter to keep your audience up to date on special events or provide general information about the product or service you offer. It's a relatively inexpensive way to INFORM people who know you in broad strokes.

Social Media is used for providing information and getting in front of people who already know you exist. If you leverage your social media assets properly, you can become a knowledge source of your industry and eventually have people seek you out for information. Not all social media platforms are created equally; we will break down what each platform is for and how to best utilize each one to your advantage when we break this segment down.

ATTENTION Phase

Display, **Banner**, or **Instream Video Advertising** should be used when you are trying to get people's attention. These tactics are also great for branding, and targeting is very important. Obviously, where the ads show in regard to geographical location is important, but "who" sees the ads are more so! You can target by demographic, interests, etc. We will make your brain hurt later. For now, we are explaining what media goes with which portion of the funnel and whether it is creative or direct advertising.

Your Media Plan

When putting together your **Media Plan** it is very important to be mindful of where your potential customers are on this **Buying Funnel.**

How you communicate with them (messaging + media) is just as important. You must know if you are trying to **get their attention or already have it;** the goal of the media tactic used in each portion of your marketing plan should be designed to move the customer to the next phase of the **Funnel**. It all works together!

Chapter 7
Search Engine Marketing

Now that you know that every consumer goes through the Buying Funnel while making a purchase decision, let us discuss the tactics that can influence each stage involved in making a purchase decision.

We will go through these tactics with a little more detail, but will work backwards, as I usually do on the **Buying Funnel.**

So, let's start with the last stage of the Buying Funnel, i.e., Action.

To get in front of people ready to take **Action,** or those looking for what you do, but don't know exactly where to have that need fulfilled, a **Search Engine Marketing** campaign is probably the best way to do it. This is the low hanging fruit of advertising and falls 100% under the category of "Direct Advertising".

Let's discuss what Search Engine Marketing is and how it can benefit your business.

Search Engine Marketing (SEM)

In today's world, SEM is now known as a very effective way to increase your website traffic rapidly and grow your business. What is SEM exactly? SEM helps you drive qualified traffic to a "destination URL", i.e., a page of your preference on your website, by bidding on specific keywords and phrases that you deem important. If your bid amount is high enough, your ad is displayed on the "Search Engine Results Page" SERP.

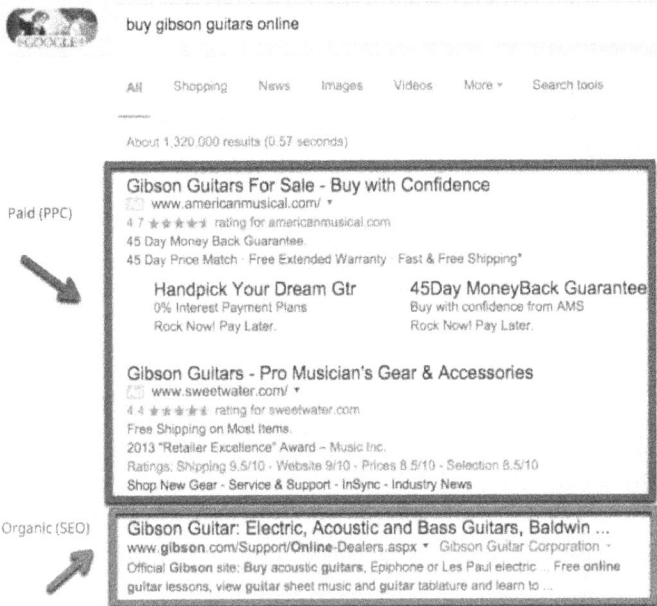

Image source: https://www.bigcommerce.com/ecommerce-answers/what-is-sem-search-engine-marketing/

Unlike other advertising, just because your ad shows up does not mean you incur a fee. Your ad showing up is called "an impression". You only incur a fee when a user clicks on your ad. You Pay Per Click (PPC). Your Cost Per Click (CPC) can range from a few cents, to $100, or more! It all depends upon what term you are bidding on, how much your bid is, and then an important factor called QUALITY SCORE.

There are books written solely on Search Engine Marketing and Google has a very nice tutorial that you can go to for furthering your education. The bottom line is that it works, it provides a great ROI in most cases, and does provide the most immediate gratification.

As strange as it may seem, you can launch an SEM campaign

in the morning and start to see results within a few hours! Another redeeming quality of SEM is that it can be a very cost-effective marketing tool.

Managing an efficient SEM campaign requires a lot of time and expertise. You need to carry out market research to determine your target market, find the right keywords, write a clear and concise ad that will appeal to your customers, carefully select the right settings, and BOTH launch and regularly monitor your campaign.

Optimizing your Campaign

You never know exactly **HOW** users will search or what terms they will use, but these **Keywords** or **Key Phrases** would be the central part of the campaign. There would be many variations of these terms that can be used along with different match types.

Match Types? Oy!

Yes, there are several ways to match terms in your campaign. Think of match types like a faucet filter that can allow for less or more water to come through depending upon the constraints you put in.

- Broad Matching
- Modified Broad
- Phrase
- Exact

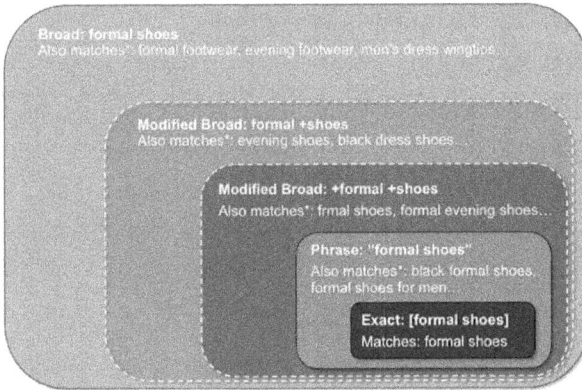

In each ring, the keyword shown also matches the searches inside the smaller rings. Illustrative – figure not drawn to scale.

Imagine these were fishing nets, the bigger nets would capture more, but perhaps much of what you may not want. The goal is to be as targeted as possible and eliminate wasted budget

Broad Match will allow for the most variation. This will pull in many impressions, but may not always be the right thing for your business, especially if you are looking to be as efficient as possible.

You will notice two levels of modified broad. The larger area in the picture for modified broad only modifies one word. The second modifies two words. Note the difference in the types of matches it brings up.

I typically suggest a start with Modified Broad and then refine as the campaign runs. Modified Broad puts in a conditional qualifier. You MUST have the terms with the + sign appear in the user's query for your ad to come up. Otherwise, it will not show an impression.

Phrase match requires the search matches with the exact phrase you enter, but can have other words around it, while Exact match needs to match EXACTLY.

Another way to optimize or eliminate waste would be to add in negative keywords.

Negative keywords are terms that will nullify any impression because you deem that this term means the consumer is not really looking for your business. Each month we make it a practice to run what is called Search Query reports. These reports tell us EXACTLY what the users typed in that got the ad to appear AND have that ad clicked.

We gauge the user's intent by looking at what they typed in and we add in terms that we deem "not relevant" to each client's negative keyword list.

Some other items to be sure to do in your optimizing will include:

- Modifying text ads
- Pausing ads that do not perform
- Pausing keywords that do not get impressions
- Adjusting bids on keywords (up or down)
- Make sure conversion tracking is working

I saved conversion tracking for after the list above for a reason. **It is very important.** How are you planning to measure your results?

1. You can track phone calls that come in from your advertising with a few nifty insertions of code.

2. You can track sales and revenue dynamically.

3. You can track online form submissions.

4. You can track App Downloads (or any document download for that matter)

Whatever actions you as the business owner deem as positive should be tracked. You can even determine which keywords are bringing in revenue!

Geo-Targeting

Setting up the geographic areas for your campaign are extremely important. You do not want to waste money showing up in areas that you don't service or that you could not get to. There are geo exclusion settings as well. Sometimes places are named similarly, and you want to make sure you are not showing up in the right town, but in the wrong state!

(An example is Suffolk VA vs Suffolk County in NY)

Geo-targeting can be hyper-local with a small radius, zip codes, towns, cities, or larger geos like counties, states, and countries.

Determining Proper Budgets for Search Marketing

One of the most frequently asked questions related to SEM is "How much does this cost? Or how much should my budget be? Is it expensive?

Well, the answer to all these questions is simple – it depends on the extent to which you want to implement SEM, and that of course, is something you would decide after taking several factors into consideration.

So, I typically answer with an analogy that people can get their heads around. It is not as cut and dry as coming up with a number.

When people ask about budgets for their Search Engine Marketing campaign, I usually explain it with the images below and ask them to pretend that:

- Their budget is water.

- The geography is the area of a pool.

- The ad groups / keywords will determine the depth of the pool.

Covering too much with too little?!   Want to dip your toe in?   Local biz, small geo Needs a kiddie pool!   Big geo wants Lots of exposure? JUMP IN!

You need to know what will work and why!
Drained pool
https://www.instructables.com/Draining-and-refilling-an-inground-swimming-pool/
Dipping toe in kiddie pool
https://www.thecut.com/2018/05/mister-rogers-wont-you-be-my-neighbor.html
Fred Rogers with François Scarborough Clemmons, in 1993, re-creating their 1969 pool episode. Photo: John Beale/Courtesy of Focus Features
Kiddie Pool
https://www.amazon.com/Christmas-children-Inflatable-Backyard-47-2inx9-8in/dp/B08BXVYHW5
Cannonball:
https://www.pexels.com/photo/cannonball-dive-diving-board-swimming-pool-80716/

I try to keep examples simple. If you are covering too much geography or keywords with too little budget, imagine the pool with a little bit of water at the bottom. (Image on far left above) Of course, an SEM campaign of this sort will not prove to be in your company's best interest. It will lead to lots of frustration. Your ads will rarely appear, you will not get many calls, and you will only have yourself to blame.

I am assuming that most have seen 'Caddyshack'. In this 1980 American comedy, there is a scene where Bill Murray is shown cleaning the bottom of the pool because a "floating doody", which ends up being a candy bar, wreaks havoc during a pool party. The scene is comical because all the water had to be drained to clean and sterilize the pool because of a floating candy bar, which Bill Murray ends up taking a bite of when he picks it up. (Much to the horror of the people watching who still think it was a doody!) How is this applicable? The point is that insufficient budget for an SEM campaign will not cover a wide geographical area. No one can have any fun in the empty pool in this example. It is the same lack of activity you will find with a diluted SEM campaign.

So, what is the best and safest way to go about testing search engine marketing campaigns for your business? I usually suggest that you start slowly and gradually expand your wings. Meaning, you need to dip your toes into the water and test how SEM will work for you and your business. (Middle left image above) By starting small, you would have to allocate only a small budget to each SEM campaign and test it out within a small geographical area.

To start with representative results, I suggest you implement search engine marketing within your local geography first. At least you can then test the waters by dipping the proverbial toe in. If it works for you, you can always expand and move on to a larger geographical area with a more robust budget.

As a true hyperlocal business, having small geography to cover, a small budget is appropriate. Limited budget, in this case, would accrue reasonable return on investment. There is absolutely no need for you to aim for hefty budgets when you are implementing SEM on a small, local area. Think of local beauty salons, restaurants, auto repair, etc. The picture with the baby in the baby pool above is the example here.

However, if your business is such that you think covering a large geographical area would be a step in the right direction, whether it is a national campaign or an aggressive regional one, you will not be able to be successful with a limited budget. In that case, you would have to set a large budget to meet the intended objectives of the campaign. The goal is to keep your campaign competitive throughout the entire month. At times, you probably want to allocate a larger budget than what you can even spend, thus guaranteeing that your ad budget supply can meet the search demand.

Go do a cannonball in the deep end of the pool and have at it! (Image on far right above)

Mathematical Budget Adjustments

Once your campaign is up and running for 60-90 days, you have made some regular optimizations along the way and have had some success, you can run what is called an Impression Share report. This report will mathematically tell you how much more you could spend to have ads appear closer to 100% of the time. Whatever it takes to max out Google should be multiplied by 25% and come up with an estimated budget for Bing as well. While Bing is 25%(ish) of the search equation, not all your competitors are on there, so you may see some decent results!

Note: I usually suggest clients have an 80% impression share before expanding into the information and attention tactics we will discuss later. Go after what I call the low hanging fruit first. It's low hanging for a reason. Go get it!

Chapter 8
Search Engine Optimization (SEO)

Up next we have **SEO,** which sometimes gets confused with **SEM** by people not familiar with the industry.

While there are several differences between the two, it is important to note that with **SEM** you are **paying for traffic**, you are paying for the actual result; with **SEO** you are **paying to try to achieve a better position**. SEO targets organic search results and can utilize more than just search engines to increase website rankings for targeted keywords related to the business.

Prior to getting into the "what to do", it is better perhaps to discuss what it is, how it came to be, and how it has evolved to what it is today.

When we think of SEO today, we think of where a site ranks on Google, but SEO originated PRIOR to Google existing. According to Bob Heyman in an article posted on searchengineland.com[5], we can thank the manager of Jefferson Starship, who called Mr. Heyman, the owner of Cybernautics, in a bit of a tizzy about the band's official website not coming up anywhere near the top of whatever search engine he was using ... As it was 1997, I would venture to guess it was Yahoo.

In any event, there were multiple fan pages that were coming up ahead of the new official website that Mr. Heyman's team built and pushed their "official website" to somewhere on page 4 of the Search Engine Results Page. (SERP)

At that time, it was what we call "keyword density" today that governed ranking and Mr. Heyman's team came up with the solution of putting 'Jefferson Starship' in the smallest black print they could and hid it in a black background. The band's website shot to the top of the rankings and the issue was solved. The band was satisfied.

According to Heyman's article, Bob and his partner, Leland Harden, started calling this new field Search Engine Optimization. They went on to hire the first SEO manager, and the rest is proverbial history!

---

[5] "Who Coined The Term SEO?" Retrieved from https://searchengineland.com/who-coined-the-term-seo-14916,

That is how the term SEO was coined!

The main search engines in the late '90s included Yahoo, Excite, Lycos, and AltaVista...maybe Ask Jeeves as well. In the late 90s, the main aspects of SEO were mainly through ON-SITE ACTIVITIES and included the following:

- Relevant content

- Keyword density

- Accurate HTML tags

It was essentially the Wild West as users were doing whatever they wanted to get higher in the rankings of search engines. In 2000 there was a Revolution, and its name was Google! No one knew about Google and they unbelievably gained notoriety by working out a deal with Yahoo to provide better results on their Search Engine Results Pages (SERPs). Every result had the "Powered by Google" at the very top. #Badmove by Yahoo!

Google was the first to not only use on-page content, but also use external links. So, think of external links like you would a bibliography or works-cited page that would need to be included in a high school or college paper. If your website was referenced in someone else's site as it pertained to certain subject matter, that means it was relevant for the related term. As Google gained in popularity and market share, it opened opportunities for people to make a living gaming Google's system for their clients to rank higher. Many people paid a lot of money to SEO Specialists to get higher rankings on the search engines. The Google Police intervened.

In the gaming industry, they hate cheaters. A lot of money is spent on pit boss training, casino security, face recognition software, etc. to eliminate the possibility of cheating, yet the cheaters continue to find new and creative ways to try to "break the bank", so to speak. The same thing started happening on the search engines and the Google Police got involved.

Websites started to get blacklisted for what became known as "Black Hat" practices in trying to game the system and Google started revising their algorithm. Websites started disappearing from the rankings, without any warning. I always say that I can "hide dead bodies" on the second page of Google. If you are not up top, or on page one, then you are not going to be found. #sadtruth

That is enough of an overview. Now, back to SEO. Here is a quick timeline of algorithm updates made by Google. They have some silly names for their updates. I am not sure why they were named as they were, but perhaps it made people feel better to fall off the internet planet if the reason was due to a cute animal. I imagine people overhearing others complaining about Penguins or Pandas and not understanding why!

2005

- Jagger: lowered level of unsolicited link exchanges and reduced the importance of anchor text.

- Big Daddy: allowed for improved understanding of the value of links between sites.

2006

- Google acquired <u>YouTube</u> and guess what became important? That's right, video content. Google also introduced <u>Google Analytics and Webmaster Tools</u> which helped developers and site owners know in detail what was going on in their sites and how they could improve.

- <u>Site Maps:</u> Site mapping became a big deal. It showed which URLs were part of the website and what Google's spiders should be crawling.

2007

- <u>Universal Search</u>: Google began blending organic links with news, images, videos, etc.

2008

- <u>Vince:</u> Weight was given to big brands, i.e., the "trust factor".

- <u>Caffeine</u>: This update made indexing faster.

2009

- Microsoft Live Search changes its name to Bing and forms an alliance with Yahoo (another bad move by Yahoo). Yahoo first allowed Google to pass them, then made the same mistake by letting Bing power their results. Fool me once, shame on you. Fool me twice ... YaFool (my term).

2010

- Site load speed becomes a factor

2011

The smackdown begins with the introduction of updates named after cute animals. As I alluded to previously, my assumption is that they did this to make people feel better about having their websites seemingly fall off the planet. Who doesn't like Pandas and Penguins?

- <u>Panda</u>: Was an update that penalized "fluff content" it rewarded rich content. It became a permanent part of Google's algorithm in 2016.

- <u>Penguin</u>: Focused on really aggressive spam tactics like link farming, keyword stuffing, and also became a permanent part of the algorithm in 2016.

2013

- <u>Hummingbird</u>: If your search engine was a car, Panda and Penguin would be like rotating the tires, maybe changing the spark plugs. Hummingbird was a new car! It allowed for improved interpretation of natural language queries that were typed into the search bar.

2015

- Mobile searches overtook desktop searches.

I attribute this to the greater acceptance of the smartphone. While the iPhone was introduced in 2008, I probably did not get my first one until 2011 and my parents got theirs around 2015 or 2016. This is when the world truly got smaller. It was shrinking for sure, but now, almost everyone had access to the world's information wherever they went.

2021

Today we spend more time on our phones or devices than we do watching television!

By the way, mobile searches are at about 70% now - imagine if people did not work and eliminated their searching from their desktops at work? That number could be 90%+!

How Search Engine Optimization Is done today

So today, we need to do on-site work as well as some off-site work. The on-site work includes everything from proper website setup, incorporating best practices for everything from sitemaps to website load speed.

Think of your website as a textbook that you would get on the first day of school. Many of us scanned through the chapters in the table of contents to see what we would be doing over the course of the semester. The website crawlers work the same way; they look at the title and descriptions of each page of your website and determine what it is about. This is part of the indexing process. We make sure all of this is set up properly and the content of the web page has the proper headlines and content to support the titles and descriptions.

There is certainly more that goes into it, but as this modification is being done, the site is being indexed and we measure where you stand. SEO reporting is like a snapshot in time. You can see what people were doing at that moment in the same way that you can see your rank "at that moment". Water tends to find its own level, so if you stop incorporating best practices, or change your website without carrying everything over, you could drop in rank, or heaven forbid seemingly "fall off the planet!"

A quick summary on some additional items to be mindful of:

Social signals and SEO - I do not want to get too much into social, but there is some weight to having a Facebook page, as an example, link back to your website, etc. More on this in listings and reviews in the next chapter.

Blogging relates to the Panda update - you want to have fresh but relevant content being generated regularly (as well as syndicated on your social media assets).

Relevant linking is also a part of SEO - this is some of the off-site work. Making posts, answering questions on other websites related to your business and linking back to a relevant blogpost on your site will always help the cause!

We measure **where you stand,** and **the incremental traffic** that you are getting through an analytics program. We use Google Analytics in my business, but there are other programs out there that can measure it as well. Adobe also has a pretty good reputation. Just remember.... what gets measured, gets done!

Chapter 9
Online Listings and Reviews

One look at the title of this chapter and you might wonder what an online listing is. Well, for those who do not know, a local business listing is an online profile (something really important these days) that contains the name of your business, address, primary contact information: email and phone number, along with other important details that may help your customer base find you, or even help a new customer make a buying decision.

Today, local business owners have the ability to access thousands of websites and directories to create free business listings. You need to have local online listings to enhance your digital footprint and perhaps even help with your search engine rankings.

Online Listings

I have chosen to put online listings and reviews together in this part of the project because they typically go hand in hand. There are hundreds of online directories, many of which come with reviews from people who regularly go to that particular directory. Small business owners are aware of these but may not be aware of the advantages and benefits of these online directories. If you hear the word *directory* and start to think of the old phone books, you are kind of right, but mostly wrong. You are right in the sense that like a phone directory, you can search by category and get the information you are looking for, but there are many more benefits associated with online listings.

True: You can enhance your online presence through online directories.

Situation: A potential customer does a search for your business. The hope is that your website comes up first, then perhaps some of your social media pages, perhaps a Google or Bing business listing, then what? Well, if you are listed with Dun & Bradstreet, etc., there is a good chance that you will come up; however, there is also a chance that the information is incorrect. Many directories extract pieces of information from multiple sources. If you are listed in one, it guarantees that other sites will also receive your information. If you change the information on one, let's say your Google business listing, it *does not* mean that this change will be reflected across the internet.

Impact: This is a problem. Many sites can have incomplete information, incorrect information, or no information.

So, what can you do?

There are several programs. I like the Yext program because it includes many popular online directories like Yext, Yelp, Yellow Pages, etc. Yext has a *Power Listings* program where you can submit your business information, claim your listings across their listing partners, and control the narrative as best as you can.

See what's missing from your online listings on these sites and more:

Image source http://www.yext.com/pl/cpadirectory-listing/index.html

True: Online Listings help you improve local visibility.

Yes, you will appear in the map section and come up on geographically close searches, like "xyz near me". This assumes the user has opted into allowing their device to track their location.

It is important to claim your Google business listing and Bing listing as users are more likely to start their search from there. Most cell phones come pre-programmed with a default search engine and you can adjust it to one of your liking. My iPhone had Bing as default and I use that. My desktop computer and laptop are set to Google, as that is where I do most of my *searching*. It's all a matter of preference.

True: It will help with SEO.

Yes, it will help with *Local SEO* searches because it takes into effect the proximity to your location from the origin of the search. When your business name is searched online, the directory listings show up in the results and help the user find your business.

Use this simple Google search *Find Italian restaurants near me* as an example.

If you own an Italian restaurant near this search, wouldn't you want it to come up? If you have a good online presence, you will, if you have your listing claimed, you will; if you do not, you will not. Plain and simple. Having your listings claimed and containing correct information syndicated across all of them, will help you get *found* a little more easily. So yes, it will help you come up higher on Google, but keep in mind that Google has its own business listings, and they tend to prefer serving those up more prominently. Just saying.

True: It helps develop your brand.

It does, but people tend to click directly on your website so long as it comes up organically. Branded Click-through Rates on organic listings tend to be about 75%+. Sometimes, they will click on your paid ads if you have them. Sometimes, they will click on something else.

These listings can also help with pushing down undesired results, like a bad article written by a consumer because you had that awful employee, and they blamed your brand. Yes, that happens. It happens a bit. I tell my clients to respond and try to clear it up, but do not go into a comment war on your listing feed, because that will make the bad review come up higher as there have been more interactions on it. Good segue to start discussing reviews now, huh?

Online Reviews

danielle halperin
1 review · 1 photo

★ ★ ★ ★ ★ a month ago
Positive: Professionalism, Punctuality, Quality, Responsiveness, Value

I have had a wonderful experience with Knockout Pest Control. They were **professional**, informative, not pushy and very responsive to requests. Had an ant situation in the summer months and after one visit we never saw another … More

👍 Like

Response from the owner a month ago
Thank you for the kind words you posted about our company. The review you wrote about your experience with KNOCKOUT assures us that we are achieving our ultimate goal of customer satisfaction. It is our hope to maintain our relationship and … More

✏ Edit

adam wolfthal
2 reviews

★ ★ ★ ★ ★ a month ago
Positive: Professionalism, Punctuality, Quality, Responsiveness

John was knowledgeable, friendly, quick and **professional**. Given the time slot of 9-1, John showed up right at 9! Unheard of! I could not speak more highly of a pro or a company than I do about Knockout. Thanks for the great service. … More

👍 Like

Knockout Pest Control Google Reviews

83

Earlier, we mentioned the book <u>The Zero Moment of Truth</u> and discussed that people have access to all kinds of information before they decide on a course of action. This is because people today are into reading online reviews quite religiously before deciding on what product they need to buy, or what service they want to use.

Before the internet, customers would call and complain to the business owner if they had received bad service or if there was a problem with what they bought. This provided the business some room and privacy to sort out the matter. At worst, the person with a bad experience could tell a few friends and it could affect the word-of-mouth referrals for that business slightly.

Today, with online reviews and the ability for people to comment on your business publicly, they can tell *the world*. Customers can write a negative review out of impulse and it could be stuck on the internet forever. Giving a negative review can be as easy as giving a thumbs down on a video or social media site. Look at what Rotten Tomatoes has done to movie reviews.

My wife checks Yelp, Facebook Groups *(we will discuss these when we get to social media)*, Google Reviews, Amazon Reviews, Feedback on eBay, and she does it to verify that the decision she is about to make is a sound one. When we are looking for hotels in an area, she is checking reviews on the hotel itself, on restaurants at the hotel, the spa, etc. I tell her, "Choose what is going to make you happy." I figure that will allow me to stay happy!

There are probably a dozen or so reputable travel sites that specialize in the sight, sound, taste, and going-on of just about any destination. Think TripAdvisor. The data is just a search away. It is very important to try to do the very best you can to control that narrative. There are programs available that help you get reviews via email. Then you receive them, sift through them, and choose which ones to make public. Take control of YOUR narrative! We will address the choreographing of customer experience in a later chapter.

You can have your customer service team reach out to people who have had a bad experience before they tell the world. You know how they say, "There's no such thing as bad publicity?" Well, unfortunately, this is no longer true in the age of digital transparency. Remember, bad word of mouth nowadays *spreads faster than a wildfire*.

About 80% of consumers reported that a negative review convinced them to *avoid* a particular product or service. I am not saying that one bad review will kill you. A bad review from time to time is expected. It is the frequency with which poor reviews roll in that hurts your brand. You must choose how to deal with it.

Most people do not go out of their way to leave a positive review. They always expect to get good service. Some people are more difficult to please, while others are downright impossible to please. The more proactive you can be, the better off you are. A nice rewards program goes a long way. I'm not telling you to bribe them, but 10% off *on your next visit* or *if you leave a review,* can get the job done.

I can tell you with 100% certainty that you can't control *crazy*. We all know it when we see it. It is the lunatic that writes a negative review everywhere; and for whatever reason, it has become their mission to end your reign of terror on whatever you do. Don't worry so much about them. They are infrequent and most users can spot crazy when they see it.

So, how do these reviews really help?

The good part is that you can always turn a negative review in your favor. Communicating with clients gives you the chance to showcase your business' legitimacy and generosity and gives you the chance to tell your side of the story.

There is a term called *Social Proof.* We are far more likely to make a decision that is safer. When I say *safer*, I mean when other people have seemingly had a good experience. How often do you end up going with the business who was referred to you by a friend? I would guess quite often. Positive feedback from a stranger in a random conversation about a place to eat may get you to stop in one day to try it yourself.

Online reviews have become a source of social proofing or word-of-mouth referrals. Online reviews also help with your visibility and a little bit with SEO. Can you put a price on being TRUSTED?

Key Statistics from the Local Consumer Review Survey 2019

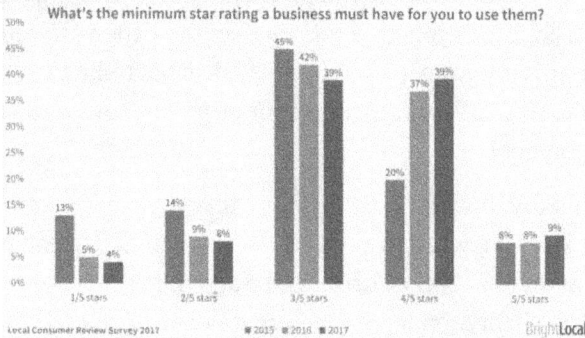

What's the minimum star rating a business must have for you to use them?

Local Consumer Review Survey 2017 — 2015, 2016, 2017 — BrightLocal

- 86% of consumers read reviews for local businesses (including 95% of people aged 18-34).

- Consumers read an average of 10 online reviews before trusting a local business.
- 40% of consumers only take into account reviews written within the past two weeks – up from 18% last year.
- 57% of consumers only deal with a business if it has four or more stars rating.
- 80% of consumers, aged 18-34, write online reviews, compared to just 41% of consumers over 55.
- 91% of consumers, aged 18-34, trust online reviews as much as personal recommendations.
- 89% of consumers read business responses to reviews[6].

Which of the following review sites are you most likely to check before visiting a business?

Based on Review Trackers' data, 63.64% of consumers check reviews on Google before visiting a business, more than any other review site.[7] According to the study, a one-star improvement in Yelp.com leads to a boost of 5% to 9% sales in the short term. This shows how even a small improvement can have a massive impact. Remember Kaizen from earlier? Regular small

---

[6]Local Consumer Review Survey 2020, Retrieved from https://www.brightlocal.com/research/local-consumer-review-survey/

[7] 2018 ReviewTrackers Online Reviews Stats and Survey | ReviewTrackers." Retrieved from https://www.reviewtrackers.com/online-reviews-survey/

improvements can lead to big changes over time.

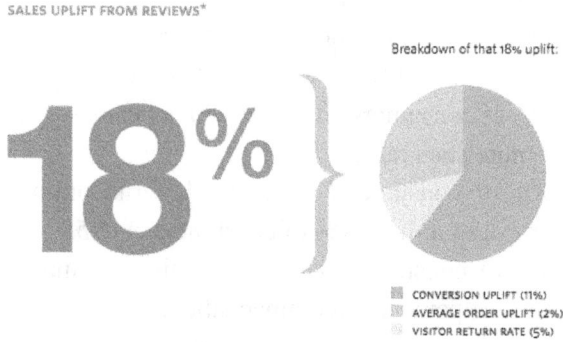

SALES UPLIFT FROM REVIEWS*

Breakdown of that 18% uplift:

18%

CONVERSION UPLIFT (11%)
AVERAGE ORDER UPLIFT (2%)
VISITOR RETURN RATE (5%)

In a 2016 study, Reevoo found that online reviews drive an average of 18% sales uplift with benefits, including increased conversion rates, order sizes, and repeat order rates.[8] A landmark Berkeley study from as long ago as 2011 found that a half-star improvement for a restaurant made it 30% to 49% more likely to fill up at peak hours.[9] Thus, simply put, if readers like what they see, they'll show it with their wallets.[10]

---

[8] "The Ratings & Reviews Landscape | Reevoo." Retrieved from https://blog.reevoo.com/ratings-reviews-landscape/

[9] "5 Reasons to Convert Every Bad Review Into an Opportunity." Retrieved from https://mention.com/en/blog/bad-reviews/

[10] "Learning from the Crowd: Regression Discontinuity Estimates of the Effects of an Online Review Database* - Anderson - 2012 - The Economic Journal - Wiley Online Library." Retrieved from https://onlinelibrary.wiley.com/doi/abs/10.1111/j.1468-0297.2012.02512.x

Chapter 10
Remarketing and Retargeting

| Visitor | Your Website | Visitor Gets Tagged | Visitor Leaves | Your Ad On Other Sites |

Visitor Returns to Your Site

Image source: https://massinbound.com/services/remarketing-retargeting-advertising/

Remarketing is sometimes referred to as **Retargeting**, and vice versa. The term has become a little more confusing as the digital world expands. For our purposes here, we will call this "Re-Engaging" your target.

With either term, the goal is to stoke DESIRE and stay in front of your audience. You want to stay "top of mind'.

Does it matter which term you use? Probably not. A digital marketing snob may get a little nitpicky and correct you if you use it wrong, but we are all friends here.

Let's define before we get into uses.

Remarketing is a term that has evolved into having more to do with email marketing. It used to have the same meaning as retargeting, but I digress.

You are remarketing to a known entity. They engaged with your website, they got to the shopping cart, you have their information and then POOF, gone. You know what they wanted, you know how close they got to getting it, you have data. So, you categorize it as cart abandonment, and you send them some emails about the product.

A sample email to this person would include something direct and to the point:

Hey, you!

We know you like this widget, and we kept it in your shopping cart. Click here to complete your transaction.

I'll use a dating analogy.

It's that guy or gal you met at the bar who you run into and they try to pick up the conversation where you left off because they did not get your number during your first meeting and/or wanted to take your interaction to the next step. You had to leave because you already had plans. Remarketing. Remember me? We were so close – we almost had it all.

Retargeting is a little less intimate. You went to a website, spent a little time there, and left. All you left was the glass slipper, or in this case, a cookie on your browser.

The company is not targeting YOU specifically but knows that your computer's browser visited their website, and they are targeting and retargeting your IP address with ads about their business. There was some interest, or you were looking for information. You either found what you were looking for, or you left because it was not the right fit. In either event, they are trying to remind you that they exist and are trying to get in front of you again.

These ads are all over the place and maybe seem to be a little creepy at times.

If we are going to stay with the little dating analogy as above, these are a little more "stalkerish". They saw you. They like you. They want you, and they want you to notice them. They try to re-engage, offer you deals, try to buy you a drink, in the hopes of getting into your, uh, wallet. LOL.

How Retargeting Works

1. Retargeting code is placed onto the pages of your website.

2. User gets to your website.

3. Cookie is placed on user's browser.

4. Ads start appearing to the user for a specified period of time.

Remember, the goal of Retargeting and Remarketing is to increase **brand awareness** and **stay top of mind** for the **customer**.

You do not want this to become white noise and appear boring, so change your messaging often. Refresh it.

You will want to be strategic with the set up and maximize the number of times a user can see your ad over the course of a given day, week, month. There is a term called Frequency Capping, which caps the number of impressions (times your ad is seen by a user) to a specific amount over a specific timeframe.

What is the cost to implement a Retargeting plan?

You can do a CPC model like search, but you can also choose to pay per thousand impressions, or CPM. In some cases, you can even do it in a cost per acquisition (CPA) cost structure.

There are a couple of different ways to do this. You have open systems of Retargeting, where *you do not control* where the ads show up. If a website takes these ads, then there is a chance your ad can be seen there. You have little to no control on what sites your ads appear. So, if you have reservations about your ad showing ANYWHERE, be sure to opt out of the websites under certain categories, or ones with content with which you would not want your brand associated.

Next, you have closed systems like Facebook or Instagram, where if you do Facebook Retargeting your ads will only show up on Facebook and / or Instagram, and only to people who have visited your website, or who's information you have (like an email list). You can target people via email address on Facebook and Instagram.

Then there are things like 3rd Party Search Retargeting where companies buy lists from search engines, i.e., "Purchase Data" on the IP addresses that searched for some specific terms related to their type of business.

What will the future bring?

I'm thinking today with Artificial Intelligence devices and programs like Alexa, Siri, Hey Google, and likely others to follow, these contraptions are likely monitoring what you say, and LEARNING.

I tell my wife that they are likely listening. She is paranoid now. I talk to her and she says, "Not in front of Alexa!". One time I answered. "Don't be silly, you think they are listening to what we have to say?"

She and I laughed, then Alexa and Siri laughed too. (kidding).

They used to say that the walls have eyes and ears. Today, I say, "There are eyes and ears everywhere!"

Chapter 11
Social Media & Content Marketing

With Content Marketing, the goal is always to increase brand awareness and interact with customers; but more importantly, choreograph the narrative of your company to the general public in the manner that is going to help you achieve your long-term goals.

Content Marketing covers a bunch, but for now we will keep to the main components:

- Social Media

- Email Marketing

- Blogging

- Vlogging / Video Content

- Marketing Materials

SOCIAL MEDIA IS IMPORTANT FOR BUSINESS MARKETING

Let's start with one simple fact. Your business needs a social media presence.

It does not matter if you run a small local shop or a big national company. Social media should be an essential piece of your business marketing strategy.

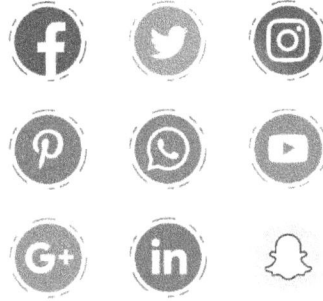

Social platforms help you connect with your customers, increase awareness about your brand, and boost your leads and sales. With more than three billion people around the world using social media every month, it is no passing trend.

What you might not know is that you are ready to get your company's social media off the ground *right now*. You do not need to know every intimidating buzzword or have some magic number of followers. You can get started immediately—and even enjoy the process.

Listed below are five reasons why cultivating a social media presence is a wise business move:

1. Create and Build Awareness

Unlike in the movies, "If you build it, they will come!" is not always the case (*Field of Dreams*).

If people do not know about your business, they can't become your customers. Social media enhances your visibility among potential customers, letting you reach a wide audience by using a relatively small amount of time and effort.

It is free to create a business profile on all the major social networks, so you have nothing to lose, but you will want to make sure you have a strategy.

LaSalle's Social Etiquette Rule #1:

No posting for the sake of posting, have a purpose!

It is better to not to post at all, than to post for the sake of it. Define what you want to get out of social media to develop a strategy. Do you want new customers to discover your services? To shop in your local store? To bring people to your website? Sales of a product? Each of these would require a specific strategy. Once you define your goal, then you can create a strategy. Your strategy will dictate which platforms are best for you.

2. Communicate Your Authority

Your authority, or as Cartman of 'South Park' fame would say, "Authori-tah" is one thing you will want to build on social media platforms

Customers are increasingly savvier today than they were 20 years ago, 10 years ago, and the millennials coming into their own are prepared to search out reviews and content on social channels because they believe in social proofs. Social Proofs are a type of Influence. Check out Robert Cialdini's book, 'Influence: Science and Practice'.[11] Great read, I promise you.

---

[11] https://www.influenceatwork.com/books/

A social proof is when enough people say the same thing to where you feel there is a consensus and agreement on what that group says. Think, '4 out of 5 Dentists Choose Trident', as an example of social proofing in advertising. Utilizing this concept, social media has created a new advertising method that uses "Influencers", i.e., people who have enough of a following that they can create buzz when they choose to.

When in the INFORMATION phase, people will do some research before making a decision. They will do a quick search to browse your website and social media for information, reviews, and other available data.

There are three outcomes this potential customer can find: Good Info, Bad Info, or Zero Info. 66% of those outcomes are not ideal for your business. A strong social presence allows you to control the narrative, so to speak.

Start by setting a plan prior to the end of the month that gets executed the following month. Keep up to date on current events because you never know when an opportunity to piggyback on news hype will knock. It is a thirty-minute meeting with your social coordinator to discuss the monthly goals, current events, and the anticipated happenings of the next month.

When we say *authority,* we mean that you want to *educate* your prospective clientele. Provide the answers to FAQs, create videos that show them they *can* do it themselves, but that you advise using the assistance of a professional. Never undermine your own "authori-tah"!

LaSalle's Social Etiquette Rule #2:

EDUCATE EDUCATE EDUCATE

If you are not building yourself up to be a thought leader in your industry, I think you are using social media incorrectly. Ads are different from content. You need to know the difference.

Setting up well-branded profiles that you update frequently with relevant content will build your brand's authority and make sure you make a positive first impression. You want to come off as trustworthy, knowledgeable, and approachable. Find opportunities to demonstrate expertise in your industry. This will establish credibility with current and future customers.

3. Show Authenticity

Customers are not interested in businesses that push out boring, 'corporate-ish' social media posts (blech!)

Let your personality shine through in everything you share on social media. You need to be original, not just a copy of what everyone else is doing! You have a mission, vision, and direction for your company. Do not be afraid to be edgy - whatever edgy means for you. My edgy is going to be different than your edgy.

What does your brand voice sound like? How does it represent who you are? Who do you want your company to be when it grows up?

Practice getting your tone right, whether it is casual, edgy, formal, funny, or friendly.

LaSalle's Social Etiquette Rule #3:

Be true to thyself, not who you think you should be, or worse, who you think people want you to be. What applied to you in grammar school applies to your business.

Followers want to see real people behind your social profiles. Show them what you are made of and what you stand for.

4. Be Engaging

Social channels, like tastes, are bound to evolve. There are newer features, and the landscape constantly changes. This can be intimidating if you do not keep up with the times. Imagine going out today with the big hair, big shoes, and looking like you walked off the set of *Saturday Night Fever*. Sure, you may look like the "*Cat's Pajamas*", but that may be in your own mind. People want something fresh. At the very least you can make something old new by tweaking it a little.

You do not have to get everything right on day one. Play with it. See what works. See what gets the most engagement and shares with your audience. It will be different. One day, it can be a great tip based on current events. The next day, it can be a recipe for a new cocktail that you learned over the weekend. (Shout out to the Drink Doctor of Long Island!) Remember, be authentic! What interests you, may likely interest others. If you just learned how to edit a video on the iMovie app on your phone, others may not know how to do it. Share your experience and how you applied it to what interested you.

LaSalle's Social Etiquette Rule #4:

Be Groovy Baby, Yeah! If you have friends that like you in the real world, be yourself and people will like you online too.

5. Be Responsive

Social platforms break the barriers between businesses and their companies. I have been stonewalled on big company websites. There are times where I have not gotten replies from suggested email addresses listed on *Contact Us* pages, but I have almost always gotten a response when I tweet @ a company brand with my question or send a message on Facebook. If they are communicating regularly, then someone is seeing the message. Part of their responsibility is to promote engagement and get back to people who engage with them.

Some examples of my interactions with brands:

Twitter: It has become an annual request to ask @coffeemate to bring back their Egg Nog Creamer. #bringbackeggnogcreamer is all me.

See the Direct message as well as the tweet screenshots below. They answered both in the same manner.

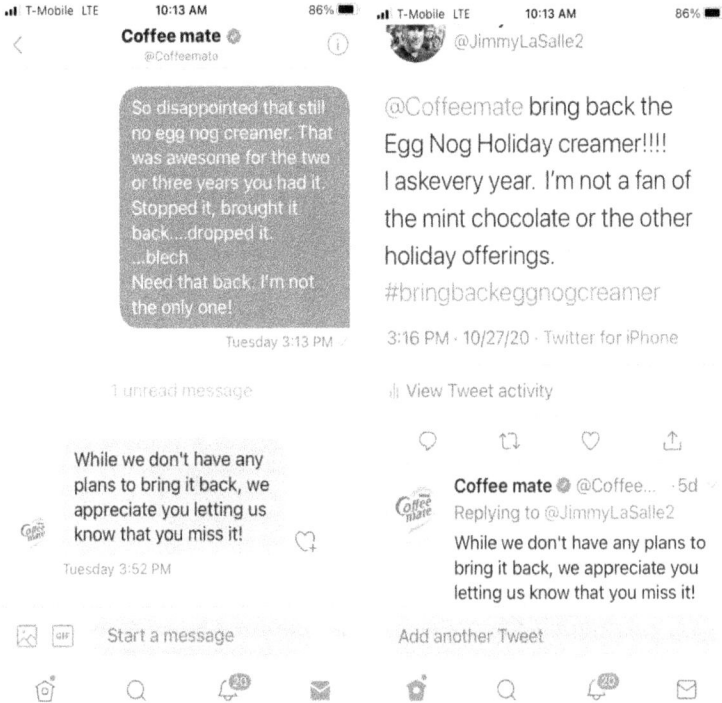

Left phone (messages with Coffee mate):

So disappointed that still no egg nog creamer. That was awesome for the two or three years you had it. Stopped it, brought it back....dropped it. ...blech Need that back. I'm not the only one!

Tuesday 3:13 PM

1 unread message

While we don't have any plans to bring it back, we appreciate you letting us know that you miss it!

Tuesday 3:52 PM

Start a message

Right phone (Twitter):

@JimmyLaSalle2

@Coffeemate bring back the Egg Nog Holiday creamer!!!! I askevery year. I'm not a fan of the mint chocolate or the other holiday offerings.

#bringbackeggnogcreamer

3:16 PM · 10/27/20 · Twitter for iPhone

View Tweet activity

Coffee mate @ @Coffee... ·5d
Replying to @JimmyLaSalle2
While we don't have any plans to bring it back, we appreciate you letting us know that you miss it!

Add another Tweet

Facebook: New York Jets - the poor person who had to deal with the #FireGase notes on every post is a saint. I picture some intern who makes these posts every day and then has to feel the wrath of Jets fans who as of this writing had not won a game in the 2020 season. I expected 0-16. They are so bad. It hurts. Here is a sample post after falling to 0-11. There are 2100 posts just like the ones in the screenshot. My brother commented and shared his disdain.

Adam Gase was subsequently relieved of his duties following the regular season. The Jets finished with an awful 2-14 record.

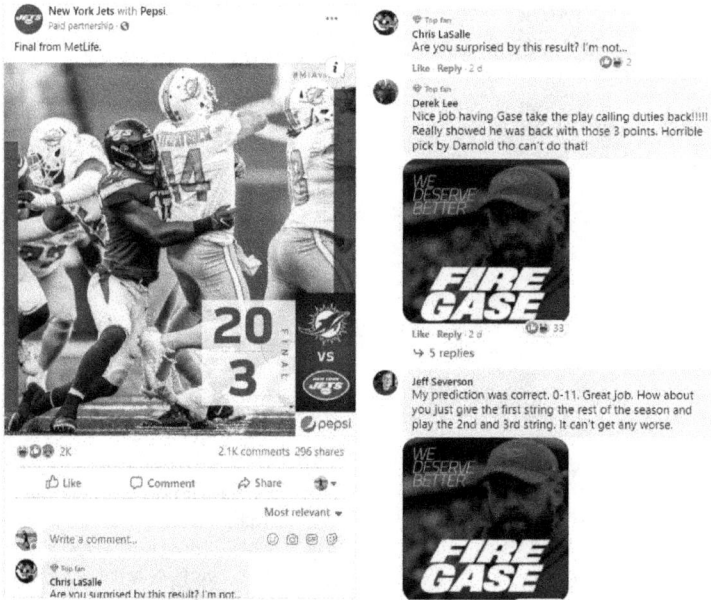

If potential customers find your people to be responsive, they get a better vibe from your company. If they get a good vibe, they are likely to do business with you in the future. Who would not want to deal with a staff of engaging people? It's like hanging out with the fun group at the party. You get a better experience.

LaSalle's Social Etiquette Rule #5:

Some things should be done in private. Do not air dirty laundry publicly. No one is perfect. If you get a complaint, solve it offline.

Email Marketing

Email Marketing is perhaps one of the more underrated tactics because most businesses hear email marketing and think "SPAM!"

This should not be the case. There are reasons and purposes for all channels. Remember the funnel. We can always go back to the funnel. Email marketing should be viewed as Creative Advertising with the purpose of pushing out information.

I get emails from brands that I choose to invite into my inbox. Why would one choose to invite or subscribe to an email list?

- They want to be educated.
- They want to be kept up to date and in the loop. (offers, specials, etc.)

This is about it. When I tell you this, I am thinking and looking at my own inbox. I get news alerts that I set. I have subscribed to relevant sites for business dealings, companies for sale, investments, brands, and channels that I follow, and I get great offers from a few golf, fitness, and cigar sites. That is who I let in.

It is important to not only create your list, but to segment as well. The more segmentation, the better. I have had many conversations with business owners who have had to start from scratch. There are plenty of ways to build a list. Social media ads and getting emails for information trades are a couple of examples.

Note* An information trade is when you tease something on Facebook perhaps; the consumer gets to your website and needs to provide an email address to get the information desired. It may be a newsletter or a blog on your website, but the information is for subscribers!

This brings me to the next subject, blogging.

Blogging

What is a blog?

A blog is whatever you want it to be. It can be company newsletters, it can be a way to promote all the times you are *in the news*, or current events within the company and / or the industry. It can be white papers in your industry. It should be educational. Think of it as your voice on your site, and current events in the company.

I have seen people create very interesting articles and tease the info, with the main content being in a PDF that gets emailed upon the user providing their email address (see *information trades* mentioned previously). It can be quid pro quo like that.

Use the information to bring people in, to grow your list, to expand the size of the audience you get to educate.

Vlogging

Vlogging is blogging, but in video format. If 10-year-olds can vlog about their new squishy toys and get 30,000 views, imagine what your business could get. The same rules apply to vlogging as do social media.

Get attention, be an authority, be authentic, and be engaging. Responsiveness is important too, because people can and will post questions on your videos if you are not clear or they have more questions. Where they see your content is where they are going to engage.

Marketing Materials

Are all your marketing materials in sync with each other?

This includes, but is not limited to your:

- Company Website
- Business Cards
- Social Media Assets and Covers
- Sales Aides / Leave Behinds
- Product / Service Information Sheets
- Email Graphics

All should be coordinated together and carry the same message.

The content you push out, both externally and internally, should have a purpose. Externally to your customers and internally to your employees.

Set expectations and then meet or exceed them.

Chapter 12
Social Media Advertising

https://msutexas.edu/socialmedia/social-media-directory.php

In the previous chapter, we discussed the benefits of content marketing along with some of the benefits of social media and how it can help your brand. This chapter is going to focus on specific social media platforms that are widely used today and the benefits of advertising on them.

Some of the immediate benefits of social media advertising are its ability for you to increase your brand recognition and improve brand loyalty.

Many business owners ask me if social advertising can significantly increase sales or generate leads. The answer is absolutely, BUT, and this is a big BUT, remember to be aware of its place in the psychological buying process / funnel from earlier. You also need to be aware of the shopping habits of certain groups of people looking for various services or products.

Below, I have listed a few examples:

1. Emergency Service: Plumbers, Pest Control, etc.

These types of businesses can brand themselves on social media. As mentioned previously they can educate with content on social media, but users are probably going to look to be *directed* to a solution (Action portion of the funnel).

Branding initiatives can both educate and brand. The timing can be based on seasonal aspects of your business. If I owned a pest control company, I may look to educate consumers on termite swarms, what they look like, and the damage they can inflict on homes and buildings. Then, when they see a swarm, who has a better chance of getting the call? Assume they will go to a search engine and search. If you are doing both and your competitors are not, they will recognize your brand as the one who taught them what the termites were in the first place.

Target Hint: Targeting Homeowners, + Married Women 35+ have been successful for these types of services for a multitude of reasons.

2.Professional Services: Lawyers, Doctors, Accountants, etc.

There are several variations and subcategories for Doctors and Lawyers. Let's look at a few examples here.

Awareness:

- Plastic Surgeons and Cosmetic Dentists can target individuals with a need for perhaps some *upgrade* to their physical appearance. Once they find someone advertising such services, they might follow the page or visit the business website. This is a good start to get a prospect on the path to your business.

Target Hint: Men and Women 45+. You can target other demographics, but let's go after the low hanging fruit!

- Divorce Lawyers and Personal Injury Attorneys will likely not have much success on social media. They offer more of a need-based type of service. Refer to the chapter on SEM for these types of services.

- Wills, estate, and trust lawyers can target people of a certain age, marital status, etc. "Are your affairs in order?" is a widely used tagline for ads. Again, this is the **awareness phase**, but never be afraid to tie in some information to educate the audience.

Target Hint: People over the age of 55, newly married and newly divorced couples

- Pediatricians would probably be successful with some awareness and informative types of ads. Push the content and boost posts that will help those people who are expecting and inform them of *what to expect* in their situation. Target such ads locally but know that people outside of your immediate target area can still be referred to your social platform pages. The better the content you push out, the more people will follow. Mention other ways for your customers to follow and reach out to you so they can always stay informed.

Target Hint: Mothers, expecting mothers, and grandmothers. You can further refine the ad with interests or marital status. Some may ask why I have grandmothers on the targeting here. Expecting women ask their mom's opinion quite a bit!

The more *personal* the professional services get, the more likely they are to ask a friend in their circle of trust for a referral.

- Financial planners, real estate, life insurance companies should know that it never hurts to brand yourself, especially in your local market.

Target Hint: Friends of your Friends, Connections within your network, etc. It depends upon the specific social media platform. This should be very local in geo-targeting, unless you have a large national presence with representatives all over.

3. Consumer Marketing of Products and Services

We have witnessed amazing success in the sports and entertainment realm on social media. Consumer marketing initiatives can be remarkably successful on social platforms because you can break your market into segments. Forget about having one video ad for different segments. Have a separate video ad for each segment. Men vs. Women vs. Older vs. Younger, etc.

You can go as specific as you like. Target first responders with certain ads and college students with others, and maybe a kid's promo for families. All these ads can have different offers and calls to action. Make sure you track your results (we will get to that shortly).

Targeting and Ad Types by Platform

I once made an ad campaign on Facebook for a stationery and scented candle client that went a little beyond the ridiculous. My suggested strategy was based around the principle that there are some things that make good gifts vs what people may buy for themselves.

I explained to the CEO that most women likely have four close friends with whom they may exchange birthday or Christmas gifts.

Follow this chain: If we target the female friends, of a female aged 25 or older, whose birthday will be within the next two weeks, with an age variation plus or minus three years of the birthday girl's friends, then, geo fence this to within 20 miles of the birthday girl's location, there is a high likelihood that we capture those with the highest likelihood of converting.

(i.e., the friends within driving distance who may be likely to meet for dinner or drinks with their friend, and exchange gifts)

If you want to refine this further, target the birthday girls who like candles, as an example. This was created early in Facebook's advertising evolution and there are now lookalike audiences and other things that you can build out within that environment.

I have done consumer marketing programs for racetracks like Talladega, Daytona, Watkins Glen, Darlington, Martinsville, Richmond Raceway, and Chicagoland Raceway. We broke down their creative messaging to the ridiculous. It was something I harped on early in my relationship with these venues. They had been making one creative set of messaging for each event.

Not on my watch!

My team and I got them to the next level. Some embraced it, some went kicking and screaming, some had to be told to do what some of the other more successful venues were doing (shout out to Hannah, Kylie, Andrew, Tyler, Dennis, Megan, and Karen - you know who you are).

I really prefer the type of client that is open to beta testing and trying different things, that is, unless you have the data to back up what works or not already. If not, when you work with me, you will have that data. We did separate ads and promotions for every different demographic as well as augment their renewal program by an unbelievable rate, sped up the process of confirmed renewals, and saved tons of time and money on labor by reaching out to the folks that knew them through digital tactics.

Sidebar commentary: I had never gone to a racing event before having these great venues as clients. If you have not been to one, make a weekend of it. My suggestion is to grab a few buddies and do what you enjoy but max out the events at the track. I have personally combined golf trips with Talladega that have been fantastic. We have done the following:

We took a Friday morning flight to Atlanta. Once we landed, we got a rental car and drove west to the golf course. After playing a round of golf, we showered, went to Talladega, got our credentials, and hung out for the Big One on the Blvd, which is their Friday night party. On Saturday morning, we drove to

Tuscaloosa for an Alabama College Football game ('Roll Tide!')
We returned for the evening concert at the track and enjoyed our
usual shenanigans for the rest of the evening. On the last day of
the weekend, we stayed and watched the race, and by late
afternoon we left for the airport to fly home and were all at work
on Monday morning. It was EPIC!

My friends loved it. They had never been to a racing event. I
have brought members of my team on other trips so that the folks
at the venues got to meet the people working on their accounts.
My advice is to find the fun wherever you can.

The Platforms

Let's talk about the more popular platforms and how to behave
on each. When I say behave, there is a difference between what
people want to see on LinkedIn in comparison to what you can
show them on Facebook or Instagram. Think of work attire.
Would you wear flip flops and a skimpy top to work? Probably
not. Your ads should always be suited for your audience.

LinkedIn

LinkedIn is a business social network. You can connect, meet
people, get introduced to someone you think there may be some
mutual benefit for connecting with, and so on. Connect with co-
workers and college friends, keep it professional. LinkedIn is not
designed to be a weekend kegger.

How do people use LinkedIn?

I can tell you from my own personal experience that LinkedIn
is a powerful tool for business networking. I can find someone I
would like to meet, see who knows them, and ask for an

introduction. Six degrees of separation and all. You may be surprised who knows who. I can scroll down on my feed after getting an alert. It is always good to get those alerts for connections who changed jobs, has a work anniversary or similar accomplishments, or events. Firstly, congratulate them but also consider how you can help them, and they you.

LinkedIn allows you to target people by job title, location, industry, and more. It is a fantastic way for business-to-business companies to market their products or services to the right person in the right business field. You know who you are looking for in a particular company. I do not care if it is the CEO, CFO, director of purchasing, or the electrical engineer at utility companies. You can target any of them.

To create ads on LinkedIn, you can use their tools such as the Campaign Manager or the LinkedIn Audience Network to target the professionals who use the site. This will help you make ads by using member-generated data to reach your target audience. Options like sponsored content, sponsored messaging, text ads, lead ads, and dynamic ads are also available for you to utilize.[12] Remember, when you market on LinkedIn, you reach customers who are ready to do business.[13]

Pinterest

Pinterest works like a bulletin board. You post things on a bulletin board or rather PIN things on Pinterest. It is a graphic-heavy platform with lots of imagery. If you have a lot of pictures

---

[12] "LinkedIn Ad Targeting Options | LinkedIn Marketing Solutions." Retrieved from https://business.linkedin.com/marketing-solutions/ad-targeting

[13] "Marketing & Advertising on LinkedIn | LinkedIn Marketing Solutions." Retrieved from https://business.linkedin.com/marketing-solutions

and products, Pinterest could be a good platform for your business. Pinterest is great for visual searching and e-commerce platforms. It has always had more of a female user base, but it has been evolving. I have used Pinterest when looking for decor ideas, clothing, etc.

Their targeting breakdown includes *actalikes* vs. *lookalike* audiences. This includes behaviors along with interests. *Actalike* targeting is used to find people with similar behaviors. Lookalike targeting is used to reach a group of people who have several interests in common to the audience you are targeting.[14]

Instagram

Instagram, like Pinterest, is very visual. The benefit to IG is that its platform is connected to Facebook's ad platform, which is probably the most powerful targeting platform of all. We will get into Facebook shortly, but I want to give Instagram its due.

At the end of the day, Instagram's engagement is extremely high, but conversions seem to lag. It could be the makeup of the user base, but more likely, it is the way people use the platform. People share what they want and scroll through images and videos as they please. This gives you an opportunity to create a variety of ads on Instagram, including story ads, photo ads, video ads, carousel ads, and collection ads to add another layer of depth to

---

[14] "Advertising on Pinterest: How to Get Started | Pinterest Business." Retrieved from
https://business.pinterest.com/advertise/#targeting

your campaign.[15]

Snapchat

Snapchat is a multimedia messaging app that allows you to keep information to a closed group of people. Private texts and pictures sent can expire as per the settings of the user. Think, "This tape will self-destruct in 5 seconds" type of message. You would get an alert if someone took a screenshot of what you sent (these alerts can be bypassed, so it is strongly suggested that you only send sensitive items to people you can trust). Snapchat is great for branding plays as the consumers are a little younger and are developing their taste. See if it applies to you, but this is currently lower on the totem pole in my recommendations to clients.[16]

Twitter

Twitter is a microblogging platform that allows you to send messages in short bursts called Tweets. Twitter is as close to a real-time conversation as you can get on social media. If you are not there when it happens or when it gets *retweeted*, it is gone and buried in all the Tweets that make up the content ocean that the popular tweets and 'the trending' get to sail on.

You can grow your audience and followers by following other people and hope that they follow you in return. I find it to be a little limited in its targeting. You can use audience targeting to serve ads based on conversations, events, interests, movies and TV shows, keywords, follower lookalikes, and engagement. The

---

[15] Advertising on Instagram | Instagram for Business." Retrieved from https://business.instagram.com/advertising/
[16]. "Snapchat Ads | Snapchat for Business." Retrieved from https://forbusiness.snapchat.com/

ad platform itself is not as good as Facebook and certainly not to a marketer like me. At least not today.

It does have its benefits, however. You can target users by the type of people they are following, age, gender, location, etc.[17]

Parler

I am not going to spend too much time on Parler. It is very similar to Twitter, but with different terminology. Parleys instead of tweets and echoes vs retweets. Advertising there is new, and I like to wait and see usage over time and see how it goes. It has built a following amongst conservatives, right-leaning publications, and Republican politicians. Let's assume it is going to be "Twitterish" in its advertising future for now. More to follow. You can always follow me on my social media accounts and blogging initiatives. There is always more to learn!

Facebook

My favorite platform for advertising, mainly because of the user data available to me as a marketer, is Facebook. It is the fourth most visited site in the world as of October 2020 on *The top 500 sites on the web.*[18]

---

[17] Anon. n.d. "Twitter Ads Targeting." Retrieved from https://business.twitter.com/en/advertising/targeting.html
[18] Anon. n.d. "Alexa - Top Sites." Retrieved from https://www.alexa.com/topsites

Facebook is where people go to stay on top of what their friends and acquaintances are up to. You can check in, view from afar, maybe stalk some exes, or do whatever you like. Facebook has built up a profile on all its users over their Facebook lifetimes. It is the platform that the movie, *The Social Network* was based on. On Facebook, you can target the ridiculous; there is no other way to put it. If you want to target married women who are 35 years of age and over, within a geographical area, and who own homes for home service companies, you can. You can do retargeting on Facebook and target people who have been to your website within the past x number of days.

With Facebook, you can target core audiences (based on criteria such as age, interests, geography, and more), custom audiences (people who have engaged with your business, online or offline), and lookalike audiences (people whose interests are similar to those of your best customers).[19]

The ad formats you can use on Facebook depend on your advertising objective. You can choose from image ads, video ads, slideshow, carousel ads, lead ads, etc.[20]

I have provided a description of some of the more popular social platforms and some of the best ways to target users on each. I also provided links in the footnotes to find the source material to help you if you wish to do it on your own. I have done this for a living for the entire time digital media has been in existence. It will continue to evolve and grow, so education will be ongoing.

---

[19] "Facebook Advertising Targeting Options | Facebook for Business." Retrieved from https://www.facebook.com/business/ads/ad-targeting

[20] "Types of Facebook Ad Formats | Facebook Business Help Centre." Retrieved from https://www.facebook.com/business/help/1263626780415224?id=802745156580214

Chapter 13
Programmatic Advertising

Image credit: TarikVision | Getty ImImage credit: TarikVision | Getty Images

Programmatic Advertising is one of the least understood digital media tactics. It seems much more confusing than it actually is. I will define some terms for you and do my best to make this as simple as possible. To make it simpler, I went and found some visuals and other resources online. The goal is to help you understand the process, how it works, and how it can work for you.

Programmatic advertising is the process of automating the buying and selling of ad inventory in real-time through an automated bidding system. Programmatic advertising enables brands or agencies to purchase ad impressions on publisher sites or apps within milliseconds through a sophisticated digital ecosystem.

Think of this as the stock market. You are trying to buy or sell equities at a certain price. These rates fluctuate constantly. The same holds for programmatic advertising auctions. The stock market works through a system of buyers and sellers, or rather, supply and demand. Want to buy some stock? Someone better be selling the shares you want to buy, or you need to bid higher to entice someone to sell. A true market. We will get into some pricing factors later. You must understand the marketplace first.

Now, in the stock market, you need a platform to take part in the investment community. (Think TD Ameritrade, Schwab, etc.) The same holds true to buy programmatically. The platforms that you would use to purchase ad space are called Demand-Side Platforms or DSPs. An example of a DSP is a company called The Trade Desk. It is publicly traded under the ticker TTD and is currently one of the largest DSPs in the world.

A *DSP* is a system that allows buyers of digital advertising inventory to manage multiple ad exchange and data exchange accounts through one interface. A *Supply-Side Platform, or SSP,* is where the publishers fill their inventory and get compensated for the placement of the ad. The DSPs grant you access to all the networks and the publisher sites that opt into their platform.

Popular examples:

- Google Display Network: Google is its own DSP but shares access to its display network across other DSPs. I can buy Google display ads through the Google Ad system, and I can also purchase them through a platform like The Trade Desk. The Trade Desk gets an API connection to Google's platform and voila, access to their ad network.

- Facebook Ad Manager: Facebook ad manager is technically a DSP, but only to manage the inventory on Facebook. Facebook is a closed advertising system.

- Google AdSense: Google AdSense is a program that Google created to enlist many publishers to join in order to share the audience of the Google network. These publishers make money when ads are placed on their websites. It would be difficult to fill the inventory for every visitor without the help of the DSP. AdSense acts as an SSP, compensates the publishers, and Google takes about 40% off the top for their fees. Not bad a bad deal for Google.

Example: Somewhere out there is a blogger who writes about a certain topic, let's say golf. They create space on their website that allows for advertising to get filled in.

Over the course of time, this publisher starts to develop a bit of a cult following. A guy like me starts to follow their writings, videos, etc. I receive alerts whenever a new one is published. Sometimes I share these with my friends if I think they would like the content. The site owner knows how much traffic he gets to his website every day.

Traffic multiplied by the number of spaces for ads = total supply. This can be one site, group of sites, entire network, etc. When I go to a golf article, the ad server knows the content is related to golf, and I am likely a golf enthusiast. I may see ads for golf clothing, golf clubs, golf instructional materials, or even golf trips. Every Internet Service Provider (ISP) keeps track of your browsing history. Just because you clear it on your device, does not mean it is erased forever! Keep that in mind for your casual browsing.

By the way, this is an example of *contextual targeting*. You can target broadly like *sports* or specifically like *golf*.

Types of Targeting

- Audience Targeting: Targets specific demographic data, behaviors, interests. This data could be gender, age, education, while interests could be NFL, gardening, or golf. There are third party data companies that provide this information to the DSPs

- Retargeting: Targeting people who have been to your site. We covered this earlier.

- Geo-Fencing: Targeting people within a certain vicinity. You could effectively target the people who went to Yankee Stadium with ads while they are in attendance. (i.e., with ads for the concession shops) This is great for mobile campaigns.

- Managed Placements / Website / App Targeting: This is when you know who your audience is and where they already go. You select the websites from a list. Let's say you are TD Ameritrade looking for people to invest on your platform. You may want to target mobile devices and people that view Yahoo Finance, Bloomberg, CNBC.com, etc.

- Contextual: It is mentioned above, but again, you can target sites that have content related to certain themes.

Image credit:https://nextleveldigitalsolution.com/targeted-advertising-2/behavioral-targeting/

You can do variations of these. Let's say you are a financial planner, and you want to target people in three zip codes who are reading up on investments or personal finance management. You could do contextual + geo-fence targeting. Throw in an age range for the people who are likely to enlist the services of a financial planner.

Top Channels

The top six programmatic channels include Display, Video, Social, Audio, Native, and Digital Out of Home (DOOH). We will get into some of these in greater detail later. Specifically Display & Video. We already covered social advertising.

- Display Ads: Banner ads.

- Video: Think TV Commercials but online.

- Social: Think Facebook, Twitter, etc.

- Audio: Think radio spots but while you are listening to music, podcasts, etc.

- Native Ads: These are a little misunderstood. Think Advertorial or Sponsored Content that looks like a news report but is an ad.

- DOOH: This can be tourist attractions being pushed out at airports or a digital billboard promoting Broadway shows while stuck in traffic in NY. Be on the lookout for these in your travels. Ever see a video in a NY Taxi or at the gas pump? There are more of these around than you know!

I know I oversimplified these channels, but this is all you

probably need to know at this point, and if you want more information, check out the link below the image and you can go a little further down the rabbit hole.

Imagecredit:https://learnadoperations.com/top-6-programmatic-advertising-channels/

Determining Price

Real-time bidding is one of the setting options for *how* you wish to buy this advertising inventory. It is also the most popular by a wide margin. We will keep to this one as it speaks to 99.9% of our audience.

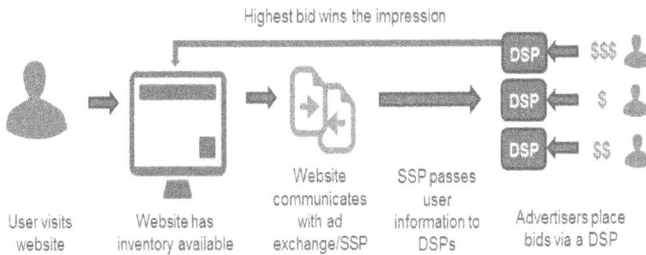

https://instapage.com/blog/demand-side-platform

Everything here is an auction. If you bid too low, your ads may not get served. If your budget is not high enough, you won't be able to have the repeated impressions needed to get people's attention. You are typically bidding at a CPM level (Per 1000 impressions), or at a CPA (Cost per acquisition).

The math on a CPA = Ad Cost / Number of Actions.

The number of actions can be lead forms, click-to-call leads, or purchases. It is any action that you deem as positive. It can be app installs, desktop downloads, whatever you want to measure. The true cost is similar to what happens in Paid Search. The winner of the auction pays $0.01 more than the second-place bidder. You can bid $100/CPM, but if second place is $6, then you will pay $6.01 for 1000 impressions, per Acquisition, or per click.

My preference is CPM because I feel that you get a better price for the results over time. So long as I am optimizing my audience over time, the CPM will come to a level that I will be happy with. Compensation drives behavior. I feel that CPM reduces the risk of ad fraud.

CPC has the worst reputation, but the highest risk is through CPA. Have you ever been in an app and suddenly, you accidentally hit something, your app store opens, and asks you to verify / allow the download? It happens so fast; I may even need to delete the app from my phone. This is an example of a bad download, but someone just paid a few bucks for that.

Dynamic CPM is the way to go. You end up with the best price point possible and reduce risk of fraud.

What is the goal here?

I'll refer back to our funnel. Programmatic Display is at the very top of the funnel. The goal is to get people's attention and to build awareness. That said, how do we know if it is working? I'd like to take a little bit of time explaining lead attribution.

Lead Attribution is the way that advertising results are assessed across all the channels that an advertiser is using to reach his audience. Now, there are several ways to judge.

- Single Source: (First or last touch point) - This could be a data sheet that a sales rep emailed to them in prospecting, or the email soliciting them for a webinar they signed up for. It can be a google search, or the street fair where they gave you an email to enter a raffle.

- Multi-source: Each contributing channel is given credit for the conversion. This maps the entire journey the customer took. There are different variations of this, but it's essentially a team effort.

- Weighted Attribution: This assigns a percentage of the revenue generated based off the multi-channel rules created by the advertiser.

Sound confusing? It can be, but this is why we have our data analysts. More on these when we delve into Customer Experience Management later.

Video Advertising, a Slightly Deeper Dive

The popularity of programmatic ads continues to grow as video continues to become one of the most preferred mediums of content consumption. Digital video ad spend in the US alone is predicted to grow up to $22.18 billion in 2021.

There are three main kinds of video ads:

1. In-stream ads: These ads appear in the video player itself. For instance, the advertisements that are run before a YouTube video are called in-stream ads. There are three types of in-stream ads, pre-roll, mid-roll, post-roll.

- Pre-roll: Ads appear prior to the video playing.

- Mid-roll: Mid-roll ads run in the middle of the content and are notorious for interrupting the viewing experience. It's kind of like a commercial break, but not always at a time that makes sense. Very random.

- Post-roll: Post-roll ads appear after the video ends - does anyone even watch them?

YouTube is the most popular video website, so I will briefly explain the pricing structure, at least as of this writing:

- Not 'skippable': Users can't skip the ad and you pay per 1000 impressions or CPM.

- 'Skippable': Most common form. You pay *per view* and a charge is incurred at completion or 30 seconds, whichever happens first.

- Video in Search: It is a form of Pay Per Click Advertising, similar to how Google's SEM works. This format allows you to target users based on their keyword search within YouTube. If you want your video to come up, it comes up in the shaded area just like it does in the Sponsored Link Section in a Paid Search Program.

2. Out-stream Ads: Out-stream ads appear between online articles. They can be pop-up windows or show within the content.

3. *In-display ads:* These videos are not displayed within a video player but are embedded within display ads or search results.

Display Ad Creation and Video Production, a Slightly Deeper Dive

Viewers Retain 95% of a message when they watch it in a video, compared to 10% when reading it in text.

If that statement does not get your attention, then I can't help you take an interest in video. We mentioned some of the tactics above. I want to make sure I communicate the relative ease of creating video assets.

An inexpensive way of creating Video Content without having to utilize an entire film crew is by grabbing some software packages that will help you create animated videos. These can run from $500 - $1500 a year.

Get the $650 - $1000 packages, they are totally worth it. You can stand out with an Animated Video with a whiteboard style or business style with some variations and characters that you can choose from. That may be all you need.

You can also create live-action videos with a smartphone. The camera quality is HD, so long as you film horizontally. My daughter has created amazing videos for me for well over a year, and she is currently 13 as of this writing. There are video apps that come with your iPhone, iMovie as an example, that help you edit and create transitioning effects to move your story forward. Script it out and get it done!

These videos, both the animated and live action, are perfect to put on your website, social media assets, or to use in digital campaigns. You can send these out in emails when the client asks for more information about your business, as part of an email blast, or use them to loop on monitors at tradeshows and other events.

We help our clients create a script and execute the production. Of course, we charge for these services, but most of this can be done on your own. That said, I can watch a video about putting on a new roof, but I am calling someone to do it for me.

Add a video to your website and stand out!

Chapter 14
The Website, AKA "The Destination" and RASCIL Factors

When it comes to websites, all websites created today should be responsive in their design. The website is a window into your business and these days, windows tend to have different shapes. You have the desktop screens, laptop screens, tablet screens, and mobile screens. In many cases, it is the first impression that a potential customer has of your business.

Responsive Design is the latest technology as far as formats for websites go. The display will reconfigure itself for whatever screen that the *Individual User* is viewing when they visit your URL. This means that the site will lay out differently on a phone vs. a tablet vs a desktop.

Does your website look like it was built in 1996? How about 2012? 2016? All are ancient in website terms. Websites should be like cars; you want to update yours every 3-5 years. There are always new things that can be incorporated into your website to provide for a better user experience. Online chat functionality, as an example, has gained popularity because it allows for immediate gratification. Online chat has become a service that you can install in any website and can be coded in.

The cost of websites is going to come down to the sheer size of the website plus functionality, i.e., what you want it to do. There are several types of websites, but most will fall into the brochure, blogging / content management system, ecommerce, or a hybrid of sorts. There are a few others, but for our purposes, we will keep to the 97%.

Brochure websites

You have your very basic, informational website, which will have information about the company, its services, and some ways to contact the business. The pricing will vary on the type of design and how many pages of content you have. Very simple. This probably makes up most of the business websites out there.

E-commerce websites

You have products to sell, you can create a simple website with templates used at companies like Shopify or BigCommerce, but you are limited to the designs they have. You can use content management system websites like the ones listed at wpbeginner.com that give you the pros and cons of each. There are a bunch listed, including WordPress, which has gained in popularity due to its open-source code and the availability of plug-ins for relatively easy functionality installation.

https://www.wpbeginner.com/showcase/best-cms-platforms-compared/

At the end of the day, any e-commerce website is going to be database driven. Your fields can include anything from images to descriptions, titles, colors, etc.

Ecommerce sites should have all the following, at a minimum. After all, you want this to work for you and you can have someone like me do your marketing while you are checking in on the business from a beach somewhere (I enjoy working from the golf course when possible and believe in enjoying life's great moments whenever we can!)

- Content management capabilities, as mentioned above

- Promotion and discount code tools

- An easy-to-use checkout / shopping cart system

- Search engine optimized code and layout

- Reporting

- An integrated blog or articles section that can be syndicated to your email list and will help you get additional traffic to your site.

- Email marketing integration - to automate your email list management

- Multiple payment options (Credit card, PayPal, PO, Terms, etc.)

- The ability to scale

- Integration with other social media platforms that can help you sell items[21]

For the source of the list and more information on e-commerce musts, visit the link referenced below.

---

[21] "Ecommerce Website Features (Comprehensive List) - Ecommerce Features for Websites & Online Stores." Retrieved from.
https://www.outerboxdesign.com/web-design-articles/ecommerce_features

Directory Websites

You have websites that are essentially directories, which are similar to ecommerce in that they are database driven. There is a template that each item, person, business, etc. get plugged into. These usually have some kind of search capability and the owners of these sites tend to try to monetize their directory by having some other kind of hook that will help them get traffic to the site as a benefit to their directory advertisers.

You can check out one of my websites, https://www.storiesoftheink.com/. This is an online video project I have created. All Tattoo Parlors in the country have a free listing and can expand on their services, provide images or videos of their work. I want to build a community. It's not solely a directory site, but all episodes are embedded via YouTube video within *iframes*. This is a niche directory as it only focuses on Tattoo Parlors, Artists, etc.

Larger directories like DNB, Manta, Yelp, and others, house business directories and contain an online business profile for most companies in the country. There are thousands of online directories that focus on thousands of different things.

Web Applications *(to later be converted to or used as mobile applications)*

More often than not, most mobile applications begin their lives as a web application. It is easier from a design and revision standpoint to do it in this manner. Chances are that you are going to want this built into the backend of your website as a client portal anyway. Think of your insurance company, Apple, your financial investment platform, etc.

Data needs to be protected. As such, it can't be protected if it lives directly on the website. Therefore, there are things like APIs that will bridge the data to the view that the user sees vs. protected data, which can only be viewed after validation of the user's identity, and backend functions that occur behind the wall. Think of user bids and data on eBay that get displayed to the user, but not to everyone. Think of the trades that happen when you put an order into your TD Ameritrade, Schwab, Robinhood, etc., investment applications.

The individual user gets access to their data, but not anyone else's. These can range from fun, gaming applications, word games (such as 'Words with Friends') to the more serious financial apps for people to trade investments.

That covers the types of websites, but what are some key marketing elements that really need to be considered when putting it all together?

There is an acronym for the key factors to include, called R.A.S.C.I.L. (ras·cal/ˈrask(ə)l, pronounced like the mischievous child, or "little rascal".

R.A.S.C.I.L.

Alright, so now I am going to share some training from my Yellow Page days. During our sales training, we were taught to design effective ads. It included things like making sure any faces were looking to the inside of the ad and not facing out, it included how to create effective headlines, and lots more. One of the most important things about ads created for direct advertising is making sure there are calls to action. You are walking a fine line in designing website layouts because not everyone is ready to act, right?

Revert to the Funnel discussed previously as well as different types of advertising.

RASCIL Factors speak to the information that people can find on a website or ad and why it is important to consider carefully which are appropriate for your business.

Exercise: Think of any business. If you own one, use yours.

Review the website and think of the customer, in this case the user, and what they are likely looking for when they get there. The customer might have questions that they need answered (perhaps they are still in the INFORMATION OR DESIRE phases). The more of these that can be answered when looking at the website, the better chance the business has of getting the phone call.

The acronym is **RASCIL:**

UNIFIED MARKETING STRATEGY

R	**Reliability** • How many years are they in business? This is important for people to know that they're not a fly-by-night company. • How big is the company? • What kind of insurance do they have? • Are there reviews? Testimonials? • Are there social media icons? Do they post regularly? • Are they licensed and insured?
A	**Authorized Sales and Service** • What kind of brand names? • What services are offered?
S	**Special Features** • Payment methods / credit cards: People may want to pay with a credit card. If the credit card logos are not on your website, but on your competitors, guess who gets the call? • 24-hour emergency service. • Pick up / Delivery
C	**Completeness of Service** • Does it include free estimates? • The variety of service solutions. • Is there special equipment they have? • Is there any warranty or guarantee?
I	**Illustrations, Logo / Emblem** • What kind of illustrations do they have on their website? Pictures can say a thousand words. • People don't like to read, but if it is bulleted with some pictures that will speak to the points better. • Video: moving pictures and video can really capture people's attention and engage.
L	**Locations & Area Served** • Be very clear on laying out the area that you service. Are you local, national, or international? • Maybe it is New York, maybe just Long Island, maybe just a couple of towns. Be clear. You can eliminate what you don't want, which is just as important. You'll want to make sure this is on the Website. • Easy to find phone number or other ways to contact • Hours and days of the week that you're open • Directions to your business - if you want to make it really easy, put a link that they can click on with their phone and it opens the GPS app (best way to do this is either embed the link in your address with a button to click for directions)

I share RASCIL with you because I have increased advertising results by up to 20% by incorporating some minor adjustments to the website. Answer the questions that people have before they make the call, and it increases your chance of winning. End of story.

Your website is likely to be the first impression newest users have of your company. Make sure all the links are working. Make sure you have the proper links to social channels, and that they are easy to find. Have a contact form.

Make the phone number *easy* to find! I can't tell you how frustrating it is to have trouble finding the phone number on a website. Have an offer that is *special* to internet customers. These can be the same offers you always run. Make them easy to find.

Free *estimates* and *guarantees* on work are always great. Try to be as easy as possible to do business with.

Chapter 15
Sales Processes

I thought long and hard about adding this segment. In all honesty, this can be a book unto itself, but sales are an integral part of marketing, and so is customer experience management. We will get into the latter next.

Everything from your marketing to sales to the customer experience is interrelated.

For example, you are a business owner and have spent some money on advertising. Now the leads are coming in as you planned, but who is handling them and how? Do they know your processes? Do they know your product? Do they know your company's history and story as you would tell it? Do they know what questions to ask of the customer to qualify them as actual customers? Do they present your product the proper way?

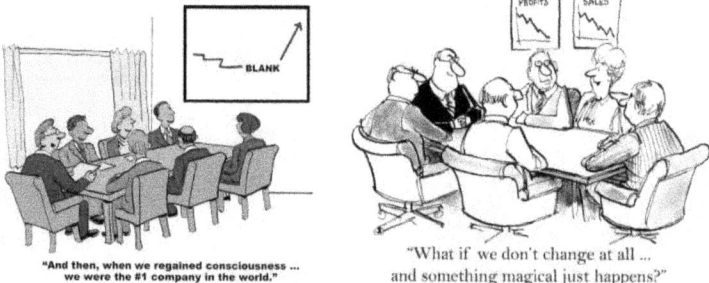

"And then, when we regained consciousness ... we were the #1 company in the world."

"What if we don't change at all ... and something magical just happens?"

https://www.phoneburner.com/blog/11-funny-sales-cartoons/

Needless to say, the business owner is typically the best salesperson for the company, but as your business grows, you have to pass the reigns.

The good news is that sales is a process, and you can 100% control that process. The goal here is to provide the process and lyrics to use, then let your salespeople adapt their personalities to the process set, and over time make it their own.

Why is there a process?

There is a process because, otherwise, there is anarchy. There is nothing worse than a salesperson that does not know what to do next and must constantly go back and forth with his boss to move through the process. It sucks for the salesperson, it sucks for the manager, and it really sucks for the client.

Having a process gives us something to fall back on. It is a support system; it is a structure; it is a map to get to the promised land - a closed sale, which translates to more revenue for your firm.

Good vs Bad salespeople

I have spent years selling. I have managed salespeople, been in sales leadership roles, and hired, trained, and coached sales newbies. I can tell you with 100% certainty that half of the people in sales should probably not be in sales. How they got there, I do not know. I will also say that there are different types of sales and half of the people that should be in sales are likely not in the "right type" of sales job.

More often than not, you can identify both. If you take a statistical analysis of your sales team and divide them into quartiles, the top 25% is what you are trying to replicate. They should be in sales and should be in this type of sales job.

Imagine a world where your top 25% is your only sales team. The existing clients can work with customer support. Sales sells, support supports. Too often, good salespeople get bogged down with customer support issues when they should be selling.

There are several types of sales:

Transactional: You need something, so you buy it. It does not matter where you get it. Need aspirin? Go to any drug store, gas station, etc. Does it matter where you get it when you need it?

Product Based: You need a car, so you go car shopping. Your photocopier is up, and you need one of those. You will compare, contrast, and make a decision

Note: In my opinion there is a special place in hell for smarmy salespeople. We have all been there, and you know what I am talking about. No one is without redemption. Compensation drives behavior. The smarmy salesmen act accordingly. They make customers feel that the commission is more important than selling the proper solution.

What do you reward your salespeople for? Is it in line with your goals? I have worked with clients on compensation models and created better models for them that better align sales and corporate goals. These need to be reviewed regularly. Compensation has, and always will, drive behavior.

Needs Based: This type of sale demands asking questions and discovering if there is a need for your product. Think of intangible services like Payroll Services and Advertising. This is where you get your best, process-oriented salespeople. Maybe I am biased, but if you follow the processes I lay out here, retrain your sales teams, I guarantee they will be better no matter what you are selling.

There are other sales approaches, like the consultative approach. The Challenger Sale by Mathew Dixon and Brent Adamson is an excellent book that talks about solution-based selling, which I 100% prescribe to. It is the proper way to sell and is worth the time investment.

There are 6 Steps in my sales process. I lead in with two additional items to keep in mind as both are important, but not necessarily part of the formal sales process. I have seen many sales presentations. I have performed and sat in on many sales training workshops, and sometimes the presenters try to throw in a couple of extra steps. I try to keep it as simple and universal as possible.

The two things to always be mindful of is *Building Credibility* and *Qualifying* your prospect. Are they a prospect, or a suspect? I'll lay out my thoughts on these and then go into the main steps of the sales process.

Remember, this is a summary and can be a weekly workshop in and of itself. I will try to differentiate *Business-to-Consumer* sales vs *Business-to-Business* sales where possible, but it will be brief. Again, it is too much to cover in a chapter.

Building Credibility

When you're first talking to a potential customer, you need to understand that their guard is high, and your credibility is low.

If the client's guard is high; they're in protection mode.

Your Credibility is low. They don't know you. They don't like you just yet, and they certainly do not trust you.

Over the course of your sales call / conversation / presentation, your goal is to lower their guard, to make them feel comfortable and to build up your credibility through a consultative approach, or what we would call conversational selling. This is really part of the ongoing rapport building, with rapport being the first step in our process.

As a salesperson, you need to be relaxed; you need to be yourself. It's a conversation, not an interrogation. Speak as you would to a friend!

The customer needs to feel comfortable. Use these steps of the sale as a roadmap to get you through the conversation by going from one phase to the next phase as part of the overall conversation with the potential customer. Remember that everyone is a potential customer or can refer you to one, so it's always good to treat everyone with common decency.

You are there to help them. If they feel that, you will be fine. If they feel you are there to make your next car payment you probably won't!

Qualifying

When setting your appointments, you want to make sure that the people that you're meeting with are qualified to not only buy, but be able to buy in a relatively reasonable amount of time.

There are things that you are going to have to accomplish in order to do that.

1. Get past the gatekeeper!

2. Find out who the right person is that you should be speaking to for these particular products or services.

3. Get the right people in the room, whether it's going to be

the business owner, the business owner's family: wife, brother-in-law, whoever else is involved in the business in making decisions. It may also be an accountant, a CFO, a partner, a silent partner, or someone who controls the money.

Steps of the Sale

Steps of the Sale

- Building Business Rapport
- Setting Agenda
- Company Overview
- Probing for Needs
- Presenting a Solution
- Closing

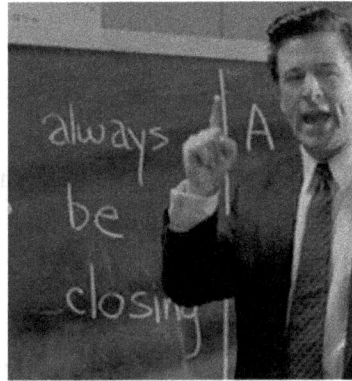

Image is Alec Baldwin from the Movie Glengarry Glen Ross

Step 1: Building Business Rapport

Building rapport is sometimes confused with talking about a picture on someone's desk with a fish or something personal. I have seen many salespeople go down the personal route and try to become a "friend" with their customers.

Personal relationships are essential, but you really want to build what I call business rapport so that they understand that you are interested in learning more about them professionally than personally. The personal relationship will come over time and with great service. The questions you might ask include:

- How did they get into this business? This is one of my favorites!

- Ask questions about their industry.

o What changes have there been / will be in the last / next year?

o Busy times of year

o Ebb and flow of their business

You want to understand their "why" for doing what they do, in addition to the "what" they are doing. This is a great time to make them comfortable with you while talking about it. This will help you later when you enter the probing phase.

Example

In addition to talking about their business, you also want to connect with people personally.

Often, you are going to utilize premise observation, look around their office, and see things that they are interested in. Find some common interests. People like to do business with people they like and are similar to.

I do not proscribe to spending too much time or going out of your way to discuss these things, but there are times that someone will take a call, or someone will come into the room and they get distracted. When they come back to focus on you, I like to pretend that I was not listening to their conversations and instead, enjoying their decor. These are great times to mention that you noticed XYZ and ask a question about it. One and done. Then go back to the reason you are there.

One particular time a potential client had a big 'Star Wars' set up in his office; I started using the Jedi mind trick on him, waving my hand in front of him, and trying to "manipulate" him by using the force.

He had answered his phone during our meeting, and it broke up the flow of my questions. When he came back to me, I waved my hand and said, "You will not answer the phone while I am here." He looked at me oddly, and I did it again. "You will not answer the phone while I am here."

He then realized what I was doing, what he did, and we had a good laugh about it. I said that I had to try. It went over really well, and he ended up becoming a long-term client. It's okay to inject some fun into meeting new people.

LaSalle Rule on Rapport: Always build more of it!

Step 2: Setting the Agenda

In order to have the conversation flow, you don't want to stop short or awkwardly while building initial rapport and exchanging pleasantries.

Using a transition statement will always help.

- "So, thank you for having me in, taking my call, etc."

- Let's sit down and discuss what we're here to discuss.

Then you go over the agenda and likely want to touch on some of these items below:

- Why you are here.

- Thank them for their time and confirm the amount of time that you have with them. It is everyone's most precious asset.

- If you have a 30, 45 or 60-minute appointment, let them know and make sure that is still okay.

- We are going to let them know exactly what we will be discussing to set proper expectations and gain agreement!

- We will review our offerings and capabilities. (Step 3 Company Overview)

- We are going to ask questions to learn about what they do, and who their customers are. (Step 4 Probing / Needs Assessment).

- We will decide on a clear next step at the end of the conversation. This can go one of two ways:

  o **YES** - they want to continue the conversation and we should put something together for them; there will be a clear date, course of action, follow-up, etc.

  o **NO** - they are not interested at this time or some other follow up appointment that you can set up at that time. **No is OK**; better to find out now, then to continue following up without an answer because they feel badly about telling you no!

Note: You must gain agreement on that last piece so that you have somewhere to go at the end of the conversation.

Make sure they are the Sole Decision Maker without asking the question. You can ask, "Who else needs to be in the room?", "Does anyone need to join us that will be involved in xyz?", etc.

As part of the Agenda, you want to qualify this person as the decision-maker. You don't want to deal with an assistant or someone lacking authority. You want everybody in the room that needs to be there.

In setting up the appointment during the meeting, confirm again that they are the person that can make the ultimate decision. (and not in a "salesy" way) Make sure there are no partners, wives, friends, business associates, lawyers, accountants, financial planners that need to be involved in the conversation when ready to decide.

Ultimate Decision

If all decision makers are not available, you would probably want to reschedule the meeting at a time when everybody can be there. Don't waste your time!

Step 3: Company Story

This is your time to explain what your company does, in very general, broad strokes. Think of it as a company summary. It must include what your company does, their philosophy in serving its customers, and the benefits of using "us." Here are some examples of my businesses.

Keen Insites Story

Keen Insites was founded in 2008 and began as a website development business with the goal of helping businesses start competing online. We have since grown to become a full-service digital media agency and customize our programs around individual client goals. We revisit those goals regularly, and then execute on the agreed upon courses of action. So, whether it's a website, SEO, SEM, Social Media, or Programmatic Advertising, we have you covered.

Our CEO has been in the digital media space since it began and has always made sure we are staying ahead of the curve by incorporating the most effective tactics into our plans.

Transition statement: "Let's discuss your business goals and see if we can help you!"

US History Repeated Podcast Story

We began the US History Repeated podcast series because we felt there was a lack of knowledge among citizens, as well as maybe a little too much apathy (people don't know, or they don't care).

We discuss important historical and political concepts that are essential to understanding and discussing U.S. history and politics. It includes topics and concepts that you should have learned in school, your teacher taught, but either didn't teach well enough or you weren't interested at the time. History isn't boring, it isn't something only some people need to know. History, if not

150

learned, is doomed to be repeated.

We want our podcasts to be informative, entertaining, digestible, and interesting. They can easily be listened to during a commute to work or even a workout with plenty of time to spare for you to think about and consider the information for yourself. Knowledge is power. Now, more than ever, you must be informed.

Transition: Let's see if it makes sense for your brand to be involved and if there is a benefit to your brand in sponsoring growth of knowledge and pride in our great nation's history.

Step 4: Needs Assessment / Understanding the Client Goals (Probing)

Asking questions, probing, or assessing is the next step in the process. This is where you're going to get all your information to put together a recommendation. You must get as many details as you possibly can about their business. Early on in this book, we discussed the Business Analysis and understanding of the "current state" vs. the "desired state" of the customer. This is going to be related only to your services, but this is the meat and potatoes of your information gathering to determine best if you can help and be a good fit. For whatever you do, coach your sales people on the pain points and needs of your typical customer.

- Business to Business: You will do a business analysis and ask questions relevant to your business services and see if there is a need for the business to work with you.

- Business to Consumer: You will inquire about the needs of the potential client and what they are looking for. If you are a General Contractor bidding on a job, you will want to ask questions to qualify, get an idea of their budget, tastes, and perhaps point out some additional items they did not consider.

This section can be a training in and of itself. Again, I want to be brief and provide examples to give you an idea on how to set up your organization's sales outline.

How to do a Proper Needs Assessment

The following are some B-to-B marketing / Advertising sales samples that need to be assessed. I always pretend that I'm seeking to open a business that will compete with them. Therefore, I want to:

- Know what it is they sell and who they sell it to.

- Find out as much as I can about the people that they're targeting, what are the stereotypical needs and hot buttons.

  o This will help us put together a marketing plan that will help them capture those people.

    - Understand what it is that they sell including all their products and services, common add-ons, upsells, service plans.

    - Understand why people would choose them over their competition. What makes them special?

  o This is going to come into play later when we talk

about ad copy and calls to action and why people would choose them over their customers – not to mention their website content!

- Understand which products and services are the most profitable. What times of year do people need these services (if that's applicable)?

- Get into current state versus desired state – i.e., where they are now vs where they want to be.

- Understand what they're currently doing now to market their business.

o What advertising are they doing, what advertising have they done in the past.

o What has worked, what hasn't worked. There is a whole slew of things that we can offer and if we already know what has worked in the past, then we can make that digital translation for them.

- Understand what their business goals are for the next (6) six to (12) twelve months.

o How much do they want to grow?

o Do they want to stay the same?

o Are they downsizing?

- Understand the return / gains on their investment, define success, and gain agreement. This is what you will be measured against. Don't leave it vague; be real about it.

- Know what their new customer is worth on average.

- If they get (10) ten leads or (10) ten phone calls from people that are interested in their products or service how many of them did they close?

  o Did they close 20 percent?

  o Did they close 30 percent?

  o Did they close 50 percent?

    - Understand the average profit on a new "unit" sold.

    - Understand the lifetime value of winning a new client. How often will they need your product / service each year? What is the average client retention time?

Again, this section is a training in and of itself. My team and I go on the road to help businesses and train sales teams on this. We also do bigger picture, all-inclusive workshops that cover the marketing initiatives, sales collateral, and processes, as well as defining and creating a fulfillment path to formulate a process to manage the desired Customer Experience. This is covered in the next chapter.

Step 5: Presenting A Solution

Congratulations, they want to hear how you can help them because you did an excellent job with your Needs Assessment!

Again, this section can be a training in and of itself, so we are hitting the highlights. I have an acronym that comes from my ADP days that I still utilize today.

SIFAB

What is SIFAB?

S	**Situation**	A Situation is something that the Customer can relate to, that they've done, or that they've experienced.
I	**Impact**	The Impact is how it's affected them.
F	**Feature**	The Feature would be the particular tactic that we're going to implement that addresses this Situation and its impact.
A	**Advantage**	The Advantage is why this is going to help.
B	**Benefits**	The Benefit is how it helps them specifically.

So when you present a solution to your potential customer, there are usually needs that have been uncovered. These can be called "pain points", "assessment points", "areas of need", etc. These will be the things you uncovered and that affect the potential customer in one of three ways:

1 - Personally - What is it saving them from personally, or how it is this going to enhance their lives personally?

2 - Financially - Show me the money! Saving / Reducing or Increasing Profits. Either way, they are going to have financial upside.

3 - Organizationally - Something that will help the company grow, be more efficient, etc.

What you are effectively doing is taking each area of need and explaining / gaining agreement on the situation, how it has affected them; then, presenting a Feature of what you do, its Advantage, and its Benefit to them, and do it as a story of sorts. Paint the picture and gain agreement for each.

Below we will examine a few examples of some of the digital tactics we discussed in earlier chapters.

SEM	**S**: You search on Google or Bing and are not coming up anywhere near often enough when people are searching for what they do and do not know where to go and get it! **I**: Business opportunities that you should have a shot at are going to your competitors! **F**: Search Engine Marketing Management Services on both Google and Bing **A**: With SEM, your ads will appear as often as possible in the geography you service and the terms related to what you do. You will now be found, and we can measure the percentage of time your ads are showing and adjust the budget accordingly. (We can talk to a Feature of Adwords - Impression Share - which will determine their lost impressions and whether they are due to budget or ad ranking).The advantage is that the business can now be found. **B**: More business opportunities and Leads can generate new business for your company, you, and your family! Very simple.
SEO	**S**: They're not appearing organically for very important terms to their business and some of the terms are just so expensive when you have to pay per click! Or, the cost per click for their terms are expensive. **I**: The important keywords are expensive and there has to be a better balance. You can't allocate your entire Marketing budget to Google! You work for you, not for Google! **F**: Search Engine Optimization Services, where we optimize your website for the oh so important phrases to your business. We do this through both onsite and offsite tactics. **A**: We can measure your ranking as well as your traffic and how they improve over time. Coming up organically for high-cost terms or high volume terms will help you defer the cost of your paid search campaigns and not necessarily miss "all" of the search traffic. In many cases, you may now even come up TWICE on page one of the search engine. Wouldn't that be great! **B**: You're going to be found. You can take some of the pressure off of your marketing budget, more traffic equals more leads. More Leads equals More Sales. With more sales, you can earn more profit.
Remarketing	**S**: People have been to your website, but they haven't necessarily called you or taken an action that you would deem as positive. **I**: You've driven them to your website and they haven't done anything, but you don't want to lose them as a potential customer. **F**: With the feature or tactic of remarketing, we drop a cookie on the individual user's browsers and we can follow them around with ads as they're surfing the Internet. **A**: You stay top of mind. **B**: When they are ready to buy, they are more likely to remember your brand and hopefully choose you.

Demonstrating Success with your Service

In the presenting of a solution, you want to gain agreement with each SIFAB. You may be asked to provide testimonials, provide references, or case studies. These all go into your sales tool belt. Creating your company's sales tool belt is also a worthwhile effort.

Step 6: Closing

In the movie *Glengarry Glen Ross*, Alec Baldwin's character makes one of the greatest sales monologues of all time. You can check it out on YouTube, but full disclosure, there is some adult language in the scene.

The moral of the story is to remember your ABCs of selling: **A**lways. **Be**. **C**losing.

Alright, you have presented your relevant solutions to your prospect. Hopefully, you have been gaining agreement along the way when you were "SIFABing", i.e., going over the Situation, Impact, Feature, Advantage, and Benefits.

<u>Trial Close - Do you see how this can help you?</u>

Gaining agreement is essential and will make your time at closing much easier because now you have to ask for the order; you need to ask for their business. You have earned the right to ask for it at this point.

There are several different ways to go about closing. The (3) three different closing techniques that are probably most prominent are:

1. The Assumptive Close, where it naturally flows from the presentation.

2. The Negative Impact Close, where there is some kind of fear of loss. Perhaps the competition is going to get the business if they do not jump on this now. You don't want to miss or lose this opportunity; this is the time to do it or we risk -----(whatever it is)

3. The Ben Franklin Close; You can try this technique for those prospects that are more analytical in their nature. Together, you weigh the pros and the cons. You're making a list on each side and they get to choose which one they're going to go after.

Just Remember, Coffee is for closers only!

Overcoming Objections

Wouldn't it be great if every sales presentation ended with a signed agreement?

Unfortunately, that is not always the case.

Too many salespeople fear the "objection," or the perceived rejection when they are told no, or that they need to think about it, or that they need to meet with someone else before deciding.

I get it. I hate the rejection, but you can't take it personally.

99.9% of the objections that I dealt with in advertising sales fell into two categories – usage or money.

- **90%** of the time it's going to be usage.

- **10%** of the time or less it's going to be money.

When they say it is money, sometimes it's just usage; you really have to drill down and get the real objection out on the table.

When it is usage, it means that they don't feel that they will get the benefit from the advertising because they don't understand how people can possibly find their business in the media or tactics that you presented.

In the case where money is the real objection, they legitimately don't have the money which in most cases is not the case, but when it is, move on. This should have been handled in the initial qualifying. As you get better at qualifying, you will waste less of your own time. You will eventually realize how important it is to qualify, right?

We will introduce another acronym to you, PEPP-C.

PEPP-C

PEPP-C is the acronym that we use as a roadmap for a process in overcoming objections. This too can be its own training, so we are summarizing.

P	**Probing:** You need to understand what the true objection is and ask questions until you understand the real objection.
E	**Empathize:** Once you understand the objection it's okay to empathize, but you don't want to sympathize. There's a difference. To empathize is to put yourself in that position and understand how they feel, while sympathizing refers to the ability to take part in someone else's feelings.
P **P**	**Presenting & Proving:** Once you empathize and demonstrate that you understand how they feel, you can share stories of other customers who felt the same way they did (this is a great time for a customer testimonial or case study!) You will present your solution again (SIFAB) and prove the value in the Advantage / Benefit portion and remind them how it will help them personally, financially, and / or organizationally.
C	**Closing:** To move forward or gain agreement.

Setting Appointments

This sales process can be used in derivatives of the sales call. We have gone through the process of how to "sell" and how the sales call should go. Isn't getting the appointment a sale as well? The sale is the "Yes, I will meet with you."

When prospecting, you also go through the process of building rapport and setting the agenda. You are going to give a brief overview of who 'we' are and what 'we' do; then you are going to sell a 20-minute conversation or an introductory conversation. That is what you are selling when you are looking to make appointments.

As you go through that mini version of the sales call, it's, "Hi, can I speak to so and so (or finding that proper person). Here's the reason for my call (agenda). I'd like to find out if you're effectively competing online, etc." Then give a little company overview (i.e., we provide internet advertising services and we've been helping businesses compete online since 2007). Then you are going to ask them some questions.

- What are you currently doing?
- How are you looking to improve?
- I think we can help you.
- Let's set up a time to formally chat.
- Set the appointment.

Remember to gain agreement on a time and date. Send an invite from your calendar. Make sure no one else that must be included in this appointment is not included. If there is someone missing, get their email address to include them on the calendar invite.

Follow up After the Initial Sales Call

After you've finished the call, you're going to have some action / follow-up items that you have to do.

Ensure you keep an active list of all the things you said you would do for the person you met with. This might include forwarding information and articles, sending testimonials, or putting together that solution for them.

Do not go crazy with proposals. Keep them simple.

If anything came up on the call requiring follow up, set timely reminders for yourself on your calendar. Remember to follow up because we all get busy and can tend to forget.

Chapter 16
Customer Experience Management

According to Wikipedia[22] Customer Experience (CX) is the product of an interaction between an organization and a customer throughout their relationship. It is measured in three parts:

- The Customer Journey

- The Brand Touchpoints the Customer Interacts With

- The Environments the Customer Experiences

A good customer experience means that expectations have been met throughout the relationship, while a poor customer experience means that something went wrong along the way.

---

[22] "Customer Experience - Wikipedia." Retrieved from https://en.wikipedia.org/wiki/Customer_experience

11,269   © 2013, Dave Carpenter

"Well, I'm not very satisfied with our customers, either."

http://carptoons.com/?q=sales_marketing_cartoons_newsletters_video%20presentations

Today, companies are starting to dig into the entire customer experience and choreograph a process of touchpoints that needs to be specifically followed.

Again, this is a meaty topic that is in and of itself an entire book, but I would be remiss in not including it with the marketing journey. Up to this point, we have discussed the marketing planning, goal setting, construction and relationships of different marketing tactics, the psychological buying process, the goals of different media types, lead attribution, and sales processes. We have covered just about everything in getting the customer into the fold.

Getting the customer into the fold is half of the battle. The other half is delivery and post-sale support (Operational Experience). How does the product get delivered, how does the service get executed?

Think wax on, wax off! How does it get done, how should it be? (Current vs Desired)

How are calls being handled when someone calls you? In Sales, Customer Service, Customer Support?

What regular communication do you have with the customers? (Hint Blogging / Email marketing)

Customer Experience Management (CEM or CXM) is a system of all the processes that an organization puts in place, all along interaction touchpoints to ensure that the customer has the desired outcome set forth by the organization. This is the future of business management. Some will say it should be the current way that you manage your business. With all the tracking available today, it was a matter of time before companies made this connection. It started in very large companies first. It is a control mechanism. We have all heard of quality control. Quality Control is product-based. Customer Experience, well, that is everything!

This is ultimately the CEO's responsibility. In smaller companies, the business owner.

The collection of touchpoints falls under the responsibility of several C level job descriptions, so the CEO needs to make sure all are on the same page.

Chief Marketing Officer: Marketing Strategy and Advertising

Chief Revenue or Sales Officer: Sales Processes and Responsibilities

Chief Operations Officer: Delivery of Service / Product + Customer Service

Chief Financial Officer: Budgeting the cost of all the above departments, and forecasting.

This is the makeup of your top team. You can add other seats like Chief Technology, Information, etc. The Chief Experience Officer is starting to gain some traction, but I believe that role is an extension of the CEO who should be the visionary.

As a business owner or CEO, you are responsible for the entire company. You are the leader internally, and externally, the liaison to the world, aside from your sales team, but this is why we choreograph the sales experience to match with the vision.

The business owner, or in large companies, the CSO/CRO is hopefully the company's best salesperson*, right? That being the case, does it not make sense to make sure a system is set in place to ensure that each and every customer gets as close to the same exact experience as possible? Think of the potential!

*Sales Leadership roles do not always go to the best salesperson, as leadership, administrative, and analytical skills are also important in any C Level role. I do not want to confuse this.

As your business grows, you can scale what you or your top team would do in just about every situation. Is this not the desired end?

We have been talking about this from the beginning. Current State vs. Desired State. Remember the chapter on business analysis? We had a bunch of questions that needed answering that were based on what is happening vs. where you want to be. Once you know where you want to get to, the rest of this is the map on how to get there.

In the chapter on programmatic, we discussed the customer journey for the first time and matching up the tactics it took to get there through lead attribution formulas. What is your formula? Ask your Chief Marketing Officer or ad agency for the analysis.

When it comes to your messaging, does it address the pain points of the customer? If you watch the video we made for Keen Insites (link in footnotes) you will see the general formula: Pain Points, Hope, How We Claim To Help, and, of course, The Payout, or Gain.[23]

The age-old adage applies to sales like it does to the gym. No pain, no gain!

Marketing flows to Advertising, which Flows to Sales, which Flows to Delivery and Customer Support.

When you control all aspects of customer experience, you win.

Look at Disney as the shining example. When you go to Disney World, and assuming you stay on property, all client touch points are choreographed. From the time you book your stay, through the time at checkout, and all spaces in between, your experience is being managed. Everything is choreographed, right down to the distance between garbage cans, and how they get emptied.

I once had a meeting at a law firm on Long Island to discuss how they could better compete online (*yes, it is ON Long Island, you can be IN New York, but you are always ON an Island!*)

I checked in and I was the only one in the lobby. I was told

---

[23] Keen Insites Internet Services Ltd. 2020. *Digital Marketing Services by Keen Insites*.https://youtu.be/de4ePm43bvM.

they were running behind, and I was about 10 minutes early.

The television was on, displaying a channel/ program that I had no interest in, but there was nothing I could do about it. The magazine stock was ok, but the issues were older, as if the subscription expired, or they felt they had enough reading content for whomever was sitting there to kill a half-hour. I can get my head around the magazines, but the newspaper was a week old.

As expected, the wait was about 30 minutes. I was brought into the conference room; I was offered water or coffee. I looked around the conference room and it was fairly bland. I sat there for another ten minutes sipping so-so coffee that was probably brewed a few hours prior.

The two partners came in, apologized for the delay, and asked me to give the abridged version of what I came to discuss as they had another meeting in twenty minutes. How is my experience so far if I am a client?

I was thinking about my poor experience along the way as I was waiting for them with a crap channel, old magazines, and stale coffee.

I opened with a question: "So you had me come in to discuss ways to better compete online, but I reviewed what you are doing and it's not that awful. For every 10 leads that come into your practice for a consultation, how many retain your services from all lead sources combined?"

I knew what their problem was, and it was not their advertising or marketing. This was to become my first Customer Experience Management engagement.

Their answer was "two".

JL: *What is an average new client worth and is it fair to say that at least one of them is a past client referral?* (I roughly knew the client worth as I have worked with others in this area of practice).

Answer: *About $20-$25K and yes on the referral; what made you say that?*

JL: *If I can get that number to average 3.5 is that worth a one-time $10,000 fee and you retain me for my marketing services going forward, assuming that the media and service will be fairly similar in service and cost, but your results will be almost twice as much?*

They were silent. I was silent. (I was not going to say a word until they responded, and I already knew what I was going to say.)

Finally, one of them looked at me sideways and said *"What?"*, in kind of an incredulous way.

JL: *"You said you wanted the abridged version. That is the abridged version."*

I said I would spend three business days in their office. They pay $2500 up front, $2500 at the end of day three. The three days should have clients coming in along with potential new business, but I needed to see three average days and talk to staff.

After another couple of days, I will give feedback about what you need to do to get that to 3.5x at a minimum and help with your office's implementation. Then the balance is due.

I'd really like to say I closed that on the spot, but I did not. It was a little follow-up and then I ran into them at a restaurant at lunch. I asked them to help me with a quick math problem.

"I know I have been following up, but I know I can help you. Here is what I got, 10 new prospect meetings booked per week

and 7 of them show up, 20% are retained, on average."

So that is 8 new clients each month, worth on average $20-$25K each = $160-$200K in average booked revenue each month."

"35% retention rate = 14 new clients per month, an increase of 6. That would be an incremental $120k-$150k/mo. in potential booked revenue, each month, correct?"

"Let's say I am wrong on the 35% every month and it works out to be every other month. That would still be $120-$150K times 6 months in incremental revenue. I don't think it is a staffing issue where you would need more people, so for a $10,000 one-time fee, you would not want to potentially make an extra $300,000 a year? What am I missing, aside from the fact that I should be charging a lot more for this?"

That was 6 years ago. They are still with me and close, on average, 35%-40% or sometimes better, partly because of some very simple fixes along with some additional touch points which increased the 7 out of 10 that showed for the meeting to 8.5 out of 10.

We set up some new visitor processes, realigned some decor, and coached the reception team on how to do incoming calls and follow up with the people on the schedule two times a day.

Upon entering, the remote is given to the guest with instructions to put on what they wish. The magazines are maintained and only the most recent two issues can be there. This is checked on the second Friday of each month.

The conference room now has assigned seating. The guest is to sit on the side facing the plaques and brag articles about the firm, as well as the diplomas and pictures of all the attorneys in the practice. They now get to see the successes and people that made up the firm, where they were educated, etc.

Simple fixes, right?

The devil is in the details, and oh, there is now a coffee station in the conference room with a Keurig machine with all kinds of coffee, or a glass of water, of course.

This can be your business. This should be your business. Why isn't it your business?

Dig in and have at the process from beginning to end!

Chapter 17
Conclusion

You cannot win in the future if you do not survive to see it. As a business owner we are seemingly always putting out fires, but I would challenge you to do a little forestry work and it will eliminate some of the fires.

Remember, if there are loose ends in your processes, or gaps where things fall through the cracks, they are the kindling that only needs a spark to burst into flames.

The more information, processes and directions you provide to your team, the better they can be implemented to achieve the vision. It is vital to regularly reinforce this vision with the short- and long-term goals of the company, and the core values of how you operate the organization.

These are the rocks on which you build your business. The business planning, marketing, advertising, sales processes, and overall customer experience are all interconnected. Take some time to regularly evaluate where you are now, and where you need to get to. Work on your business and avoid being perpetually in it because the more processes and systems you have in place, the bigger the growth.

While it may be easier to fly by the seat of your pants when you are a small business with a small team, you will not grow magnificently, and you will stay small.

When I speak with groups of business owners, or top teams at larger firms to outline these processes in workshops, I preach to start with the end in mind.

Dig in. Get the real numbers. You can estimate, sure, but the point is to know, control, and be involved in the creation of the whole plan.

I love conducting our workshops and meeting new people. I enjoy helping them with their businesses. Sometimes it is a sales workshop, sometimes it is a CXM analysis, sometimes it's the whole process. My hope is that this book will allow entrepreneurs and CEOs to begin to walk in the footsteps of their customer's journey. Learn more at www.jimmylasalle.com and drop us a line.

Everyone goes through the same process of attention, information, desire, and action. This roadmap allows us to set up the proper communication to move from one phase to another.

The mediums with which to advertise are varied. I spent time on digital tactics but there is obviously a place for traditional advertising, although this is less likely the case during the coming years as they evolve into digital formats themselves.

Work with your sales teams, arm them with the tools they need to be successful, and the lyrics to set proper expectations.

Work with your operations teams and what needs to be delivered in order to meet the expectations set by salespeople. Make sure to have dialogue between departments regularly. Sales and Ops need to work well together. Remember, your financial score is the average of Sales + Operations!

We covered much. I sincerely hope you found it to be useful as well as entertaining. All my best to you in your journey.

Jimmy LaSalle

Appendix: Business Analysis Worksheet

Current State

Score Your Sales / Marketing on a scale from 1- 10 _____

Score your operations on a scale from 1 – 10 _____

The average of these two scores = Financial Health _____

Determine best ways to increase revenue

Do you need to Sell More New Units of business? _____

How many more per month? _____

Can you add additional / complimentary products or services? (List below)

_____

_____

_____

_____

_____

_____

_____

Can you change internal processes to manage workflow more efficiently? (List which ones)

_____

_____

_____

_____

_____

Can you cut costs of sales, operations, or Vendors? (List)

_____

_____

_____

_____

_____

Services / Products outlined + Geography Served

Where do your customers come from? (Geographically)

_____

_____

_____

_____

_____

_____

What business do you do? - Define all your products and services that your business offers.

_____

_____

_____

_____

_____

_____

_____

Rank the list from previous question in order of importance.

Product / Service	Rank of Importance	Description:

Define your customer and the potential problems they have for which you can provide a solution:

_____

_____

_____

_____

_____

_____

_____

The competition and where you fall short

What differentiates you from your competition?

_____

_____

_____

_____

_____

_____

_____

UNIFIED MARKETING STRATEGY

Who are your competitors? (List the main ones)

_____

_____

_____

_____

_____

_____

_____

What do they do that you like? Perhaps you can learn from your competition!

_____

_____

_____

_____

_____

_____

_____

What do they do that you do, but better? Why?

_____

_____

_____

_____

_____

_____

_____

_____

Why would someone choose one of your competitors over you?

_____

_____

_____

_____

_____

_____

_____

_____

What reasons would you list that you can do better - i.e. what do you suck at?? (This is an important question for you to answer) Sometimes it is very hard to take a look in the mirror and really know what you do wrong.

_____
_____
_____
_____
_____
_____
_____
_____

Ask your staff what you can be doing better. As a business owner, you have to realize that you are not perfect. Your team knows your weaknesses, trust me. Ask them.

Getting into the Numbers

Gross Revenue last year, and perhaps the year prior as well.

_____
_____

What is your projected revenue this year?

_____
_____

How much revenue, as a percentage, is coming from each of your offerings? List and put a percentage next to each. (Note grid next page, Use these lines for notes.)

_____

_____

_____

_____

_____

_____

_____

How much profit, as a percentage of gross profit, is coming from each revenue source? Is there a way to focus more on what is most profitable?

_____

_____

_____

_____

_____

_____

Is there a loss leader (a product sold at a loss to attract customers)? What is it? _____

Product / Service	Revenue	% of Gross Revenue

Operations

In order to best view your operational processes, outline your business workflow in a flowchart. This would clearly show what happens when fulfilling a work order.

_____

_____

_____

_____

_____

_____

_____

_____

What are your operations and processes, and is everything documented or not?

_____

_____

_____

_____

_____

_____

_____

Now, outline each operational process of your business and how you want it to be done. Compare current to desired.

_____

_____

_____

_____

_____

_____

_____

_____

Create a flowchart of what happens from beginning to end, from the time a customer calls to the time they pay and tell you they will refer business to you in the future! Do this for each operational process.

_____

_____

_____

_____

_____

_____

_____

_____

What is your current capacity to bring on more business?

_____

_____

_____

_____

_____

_____

_____

_____

Sales Processes

Identify what kind of sales processes you have in place. Write down the steps you take to bring on a client and then ask your salespeople what their perception is. Maybe it needs some tweaking.

_____

_____

_____

_____

_____

_____

_____

_____

Do your marketing and sales collateral mesh? Is it consistent? List all of your marketing and sales collateral needs. What do you have already and what else is needed?

_____

_____

_____

_____

_____

_____

_____

_____

Advertising Planning

List all the advertising you are doing currently, the goal of the advertising you're doing, how much you are spending in a month, and the average number of leads it generates.

Advertising Tactic	Monthly Cost	Avg # Leads	Planned Goal

Make a list of advertising tactics that used to work for your business. For instance, what advertising platforms you used (Yellow Pages, trade magazines, print, etc.), monthly spend, monthly leads generated, and when and why you stopped spending money on that platform. If your goal with a tactic is branding, list it as such.

Advertising Tactic	Monthly Cost	Avg # Leads	Planned Goal

Desired state

Do you want to maintain your current state and perhaps try to improve profitability, or are you looking to grow? Describe your vision for the future.

_____

_____

_____

_____

_____

_____

_____

Where do you want revenue to be? Is there a product or service you wish to expand into?

_____

_____

_____

_____

_____

_____

_____

What business do you want to be in? Make a list of products or services to add to or remove from your current offerings, and by when.

_____

_____

_____

_____

_____

_____

_____

_____

Who should your customers be? Break out the demographics of your target audience and rank them in importance - who are your best customers? Who are your worst customers?

_____

_____

_____

_____

_____

_____

_____

_____

Where do you want to service? Should you be going further out, or should you be eliminating clients beyond a certain distance because they are too expensive to service?

_____

_____

_____

_____

_____

_____

_____

List a few things you will incorporate that your competition is already doing, some things they are not doing, and ways you feel you can outperform them. Make sure anything that needs changing or updating gets listed here with due dates for you and your team.

_____

_____

_____

_____

_____

_____

_____

Know the numbers you wish to achieve.

Gross revenues 1-3 years out _____ _____ _____

Number of new business units needed to achieve per month or quarter.

_____

_____

_____

_____

_____

_____

_____

_____

How much internal growth will your sales team need? Or better yet, how can we increase the daily, weekly, monthly activity of your current team to achieve the new goals without hiring more people? (Refer to your sales process section)

_____

_____

_____

_____

_____

_____

_____

_____

What products or services should be of higher or lower focus based off what you found in the current state exercise?

_____

_____

_____

_____

_____

_____

_____

_____

Operational efficiencies - what can be improved?

What processes will you change first? Prioritize!

_____

_____

_____

_____

_____

_____

_____

_____

Sales & Marketing Processes

This is how you want things represented in the future. Do this after reading the sales section and / or talking to your team to find best practices currently happening and incorporating them into an adjusted model going forward.

Outline your future advertising and marketing upon completion of the program and incorporate all you learned in the following section.

Tactic	Budget	Goal

Bibliography

"Zero Moment of Truth (ZMOT) Decision-Making Moment." *Think with Google*. Retrieved from https://www.thinkwithgoogle.com/marketing-resources/micro-moments/zero-moment-truth/

"Who Coined The Term SEO?" Retrieved from https://searchengineland.com/who-coined-the-term-seo-14916,

Local Consumer Review Survey 2020, Retrieved from https://www.brightlocal.com/research/local-consumer-review-survey/

2018 ReviewTrackers Online Reviews Stats and Survey | ReviewTrackers." Retrieved from https://www.reviewtrackers.com/online-reviews-survey/

"The Ratings & Reviews Landscape | Reevoo." Retrieved fromhttps://blog.reevoo.com/ratings-reviews-landscape/

"5 Reasons to Convert Every Bad Review Into an Opportunity." Retrieved from https://mention.com/en/blog/bad-reviews/

"Learning from the Crowd: Regression Discontinuity Estimates of the Effects of an Online Review Database* - Anderson - 2012 - The Economic Journal - Wiley Online Library." Retrieved from https://onlinelibrary.wiley.com/doi/abs/10.1111/j.1468-0297.2012.02512.x

"LinkedIn Ad Targeting Options | LinkedIn Marketing
Solutions." Retrieved from
https://business.linkedin.com/marketing-solutions/ad-
targeting

"Marketing & Advertising on LinkedIn | LinkedIn Marketing
Solutions." Retrieved from
https://business.linkedin.com/marketing-solutions

"Advertising on Pinterest: How to Get Started | Pinterest
Business." Retrieved from
https://business.pinterest.com/advertise/#targeting

Advertising on Instagram | Instagram for Business." Retrieved
from https://business.instagram.com/advertising/

"Snapchat Ads | Snapchat for Business." Retrieved from
https://forbusiness.snapchat.com/

Anon. n.d. "Twitter Ads Targeting." Retrieved from
https://business.twitter.com/en/advertising/targeting.html

Anon. n.d. "Alexa - Top Sites." Retrieved from
https://www.alexa.com/topsites

"Facebook Advertising Targeting Options | Facebook for
Business." Retrieved from
https://www.facebook.com/business/ads/ad-targeting

"Types of Facebook Ad Formats | Facebook Business Help
Centre." Retrieved from
https://www.facebook.com/business/help/126362678041
5224?id=802745156580214

"Ecommerce Website Features (Comprehensive List) -
Ecommerce Features for Websites & Online Stores."

Retrieved from. https://www.outerboxdesign.com/web-design-articles/ecommerce_features

"Customer Experience - Wikipedia." Retrieved from https://en.wikipedia.org/wiki/Customer_experience

Keen Insites Internet Services Ltd. 2020. *Digital Marketing Services by Keen Insites*.https://youtu.be/de4ePm43bvM.

www.ingramcontent.com/pod-product-compliance
Lightning Source LLC
Chambersburg PA
CBHW071729200326
41519CB00021BC/6636